PREPARING

for the

KINGDOM OF GOD

True Divine Encounters and Teachings from the Lord Jesus Christ

BOOK ONE

GLENN K VAN ROOYEN

Publisher: Preparing for the Kingdom Ministry; P.O. Box 340, Ennerdale, South Africa, 1826.

ISBN Number: 978-0-9968294-0-3

For information, contact:

Preparing for the Kingdom Ministry,

P.O. Box 340, Ennerdale, South Africa, 1826.

Online :

info@prepareforthekingdom.com | www.preparingforthekingdom.com

Book Editing and Cover Design by Abrams and Janet Anunda.

First Edition: December 2015

Acknowledgments

I would like to express my deepest gratitude to our Lord and Savior, Jesus Christ, for His guidance and help in writing this book. In September 2014, my family asked the Lord if we could write a book on the various articles, messages, and visions that He had given us over a four-year period, and He said *"Yes!"*

After one year of planning, in-house editing, discussions, and prayers, we have finally put this book together. By the grace of the living God, He blessed me with a team of very dedicated and prayerful friends who painstakingly read, advised and corrected the manuscript without complaining. God's rich and everlasting blessing be upon my friends and faithful brethren—the Anunda family – for all the work and time they put into this book. This is a faithful family and the Lord Jesus Christ Himself has given them some kind words of great encouragement. May the Lord reward them greatly and give them peace!

I would like to thank and give glory to our Almighty Father in Heaven for the support, encouragement and prayers of my own family. My wife, Desiree, and my children, Charis, Claudia, Cailin, and Jaydeen have supported me in every way. They patiently prayed and fasted with me, and shared my vision for this work. We pray that you, our reader, will receive the riches of our work and dedication through these teachings as given to us by Jesus Christ Himself.

Grace and peace to you,

Brother Glenn K van Rooyen.

Contents

CHAPTER 1

How this Ministry Started

The Church historian and fellow witness of the Gospel of our Lord Jesus Christ, Luke, wrote to Theophilus saying, *"it seemed good to me also, having had perfect understanding of all things from the very first, to write to you an orderly account, most excellent Theophilus"* (Luke 1:3 NKJV). In the same manner, God intended to preserve a record of His interaction with the human race for the benefit of present and future generations without having to repeat Himself over and over again. He, therefore, commanded Moses to 'write' what He said (Exodus 17:14; 34:27). The Lord also commanded Moses to record their journey from Egypt into the Land of Canaan (Numbers 33:2-51).

As a ministry, we have also traveled a journey with the Lord, and He has commanded us to write an orderly account of our journey with Him. This will be a rather brief account, and for the sake of clarity, please forgive us if we reiterate this information elsewhere in the book.

The Appearance of the Lord Jesus

In 2009, my wife and I, along with our daughter Charis, who was eight years' old at the time, decided to establish a home fellowship. As a custom, every night before bedtime we would read from the Bible and pray, with each one of us reading a portion of Scripture and expounding where necessary. Even at such a tender age, Charis enjoyed these sessions very much, and she would always remind us when it was time to meet.

As a family, we have faithfully continued this home fellowship, meeting daily, and this practice has become the hallmark of our home, just as Joshua declared *"As for me and my house we will serve the Lord"* (Joshua 24:15).

The Lord's First Visit to Charis

During the Sunday church service of January 24, 2010, our then-pastor announced a seven-day fast, encouraging us to pray for the needs of the local church as well as ours. Since we were plagued with financial debt and worries at the time and the fact that I had been unemployed for a full year, my wife and I decided to join our local church in this seven-day fast. As it is, we had been unable to pay our home mortgage (bond) for almost a full year.

During that time, I submitted applications for various jobs and attended countless interviews, yet all doors to employment were closed. These were very frustrating and trying times for us as a family. As a father, I was unable to fulfill my responsibility to provide for my family, and this led to severe tensions and quarrels at home. In my desperation, I started making plans to put up our house for rent and move back to my parents' house, while my wife was to move in with her parents along with our two daughters. In the midst of all of our problems, we still continued praying and trusting the Lord for a miracle.

Amazingly, and completely unexpected, on the night of January 25, 2010, the Lord appeared to my daughter Charis for the first time. He gently told her, *"I love My children. My daughter Charis, I am your Lord and Savior Jesus Christ. I am going to talk to you and show you visions, and you must tell your father to keep a record of all that I will show to you."* This visit from the Lord rejuvenated our spirits and marked a new beginning in our relationship with Him. True to His promise, this would not be the last visit.

We have compiled several teachings and experiences from the Lord, and we are pleased to share them with you to encourage you in your faith as you continue seeking and trusting Him.

How Does Jesus Look Like?

Some of you may be wondering how Jesus looks like. When Charis saw the Lord, He was standing on a pure white cloud (Nahum 1:3b; Revelation 14:14), wearing a shiny, white robe lined with golden stripes (Revelation 1:13). Across His robe, from shoulder to hip, was written "KING OF KINGS AND LORD OF LORDS" (Revelation 19:16). She could not see the Lord's face; it was covered with brilliant light, but she could see that He was wearing a golden crown on His head (Revelation 14:14).

During another visit, Charis asked the Lord to show her His hands and feet. She saw the nail marks on his feet and when He opened His hand she saw the scars of the cross (Luke 24:40; John 20:27). Because the Lord's face is not visible but concealed in brilliant light, she could not see His hair. When she asked Him, He slightly bent forward and showed her His hair; it was pure white like wool (Revelation 1:14).

A Foundation of Prayer

In March 2010, after the Lord had given us (my wife, Charis and me) spiritual gifts for the work of service in this ministry, He commanded me to look for five willing, born-again Christians to pray with us every Saturday morning for eight weeks. Soon after we completed the eight weeks of prayer, the Lord blessed all the five people who prayed with me with what they needed at the time. For being obedient and making an effort to participate in the prayers, a brother who had been unemployed for over 3 years was blessed with a good job; he is currently still employed in the same place and was promoted to a higher position. Also, a sister who desired the gift of tongues received this gift on our last day of the eight weeks of prayer. In addition, the Lord answered the desperate pleas of a mother who prayed with us interceding for her drug-addicted son; He delivered the son from drug addiction and demons on December 15, 2010. Five years after being delivered, this brother is still saved—Glory to God! Furthermore, the Lord also answered the prayers of a woman who was interceding for the healing of one of the children in her family. The Lord faithfully answered many other prayer requests that we brought before Him during this eight weeks of prayers. The Lord taught us and confirmed to us through this test, that when we are committed to praying consistently, He answers our prayers.

After we completed the eight weeks of prayer, the Lord commanded my wife to find five people to pray with her every Saturday morning. This fellowship still continues today as a women's prayer meeting. We can testify that through this prayer group, some people whom they prayed for and who had faith confirmed that they received jobs, healing, deliverance, and salvation. In addition, for their work of intercessory prayers, the Lord has granted peace, health, and providence to these women, and this has further contributed to their faith and dependence on the Lord as their Source of strength.

From Evening Prayer Meetings to Street Ministry

In August 2010, the Lord commanded me and my wife to find ten people to pray with and start a separate intercessory prayer group. He gave us a timeframe to find additional people, and this number gradually increased to twenty. Some of the people who promised to join us never showed up, but we continued our prayer sessions with the few committed ones who came.

After praying with ten people every Friday evening for five weeks, the Lord commanded us to change the weekly intercessory prayer time to Saturday evening, and this continues to this day. Through these experiences, the Lord taught us that corporate prayer is important, and each church should have an intercessory prayer group (Acts 4:31; Acts 6:4).

In establishing our witnessing or evangelism ministry, the Lord commanded that we, along with members of our prayer group, go out witnessing in our local community and lay hands on the sick and those who needed deliverance from demonic oppression (Luke 10:1-23). This witnessing work has resulted in the salvation, healing, and deliverance of many people, as we continue going out in the name of Jesus (Mark 16:15-18). The Lord established every Friday evening as the time for us to go out and witness.

The Lord is caring and He does not want His work to be burdensome (Matthew 11:30). After many weeks of witnessing, the Lord would give us breaks during very cold and rainy days. As individual members of this ministry, we have also developed the habit of daily witnessing to families, friends, colleagues, and whomsoever we would come across during our daily routines.

Home Church Services that are Pleasing to God

Most local churches in our community are accustomed to holding Wednesday evening services. We initially followed this tradition and opened our home living room as a place for our Wednesday evening services, but having the honor of the Lord as our Leader, He set our service and meeting times. We strongly encourage Brethren who meet to fellowship at home to surrender the service to the Lord and have Him as their Leader, instead of fighting for control. Having mentioned meeting days, we are not suggesting that the days we choose to worship should generally apply to everyone. Surely, worship times and days are normally set by local congregants within a given community. Insisting on Sunday or Saturday as days of worship promotes sectarianism, not Christ (Romans 14:5).

Unfortunately, Home Church services can serve as means to control individual believers, instead of focusing on Christ. For example, most Home/cell church services happening on Wednesday evenings in Pentecostal and charismatic churches, particularly here in South Africa, involve a discussion of a pastor's sermon or Sunday message. Having been part of this system, and being eager to grow, I found this gathering to be more of a social event than a prayer gathering. Under this system, I understand that pastors are careful not to expose their flock to wrong teachings, and the small group mechanism serves to control and protect the members. However, this system often neither stimulates growth nor allows room for the Holy Spirit to work and use individual believers. I personally believe that these kinds of gatherings could be used to more effectively develop and mold individuals into God-fearing leaders.

I strongly believe that instead of pastors exerting stringent controls, Home Church leaders should be allowed to exercise their faith so that the Holy Spirit can work through them for the benefit of the rest of the group (Titus 2:1-2). The Apostle Paul did not dictate to Timothy or Titus, but he encouraged them to stick to Scriptural teachings and sound doctrine (2 Timothy 3:16; 4:2). In countless messages to many individuals in our ministry and outside, the Lord encouraged believers to read the Bible from cover to cover. This approach to Bible reading undoubtedly gives us a holistic understanding of the Bible message, instead of just picking on individual verses. As it is, many Christians today base their faith on specific Bible verses that suit their selfish interest, while disregarding the rest of the Scriptures. This has led to widespread confusion, division and deception in the body of Christ. With this narrow system, we see people following men or their leaders for their particular teachings and doctrines (for example prosperity or certain spiritual/supernatural manifestations), instead of being followers of the Lord Jesus Christ and fully embracing His truth (1 Timothy 4:6; 1 Corinthians 1:12-13).

The Lord provides the weekly messages that we share, and He also gave me word through Charis on what I should preach about. The messages that the Lord would give me to preach would often be based on people's current situations; for example, when we had sick people, I would be asked to preach about healing in Christ. Those who were going through a crisis of any kind found answers and encouragement in the message the Lord gave. Where sinful behavior played a role in those circumstances, the Lord would issue a rebuke to the individual concerned, and give a word to me to write or preach as a warning to others. In an effort to share the gospel with the households of brethren who are part of our ministry, the Lord directed that we take turns having church services at member's homes, and we rotated services for almost two years. Brethren, during this time of directing our ministry activity, like His disciples we did not understand what the Lord was doing (John 12:16). As we look back and see the fruit of our work accomplished by His grace, we can only bow down in worship, praise and thanksgiving to our Savior for His involvement in our lives.

Following a two-year period of preaching, the Lord gave each member of the ministry personal messages, commanding us to all concentrate on reading our Bibles every day and praying three or more times daily in our fellowship with Him (Joshua 1:8; Psalm 55:17; Daniel 6:10; 2 Corinthians 12:8). When we failed to obey, the Lord taught us His Word by rebuking us strongly for our sins, in order to ensure that we keep growing in His will (Job 42:7; Proverbs 3:11-12; Hebrews 12:6). In April 2012, after noticing our obedience and growth in our personal fellowship with Him, the Lord changed our traditional Wednesday preaching services to praise and worship sessions. Before commencing our worship services, as a custom, we regularly open our services with prayer and a word of encouragement from the Bible (1 Corinthians 14:26). The Lord uses these praise and worship services to heal the broken hearted and sick and deliver those bound or oppressed by demons. At the same time, He draws each one of us closer to Him in a fellowship of solemn unity with His Holy Spirit.

Unbelieving and Doubtful Brethren

Many brothers and sisters who first heard about the Lord's dealing with this family believed our testimony due to the blessings He imparted on us and the fruit of our work in Him. However, some of these people broke faith with us as a result of their insistence on us getting a Word for them from the Lord. Many of those who asked us to inquire of the Lord for them did not anticipate the kind of message they would receive. Often they expected to receive a "good fortune", "prosperity" or "feel good" message from the Lord which corresponded with their worldly lifestyles. However, the Word from the Lord would often be a message of rebuke, exposing their wrong habits and lifestyle. Those who faithfully served Him would receive a message of encouragement. Some people were so embarrassed that they chose to leave our fellowship and dissociate with us.

In a number of visions, the Lord warned the people of the world that they have received and believed another gospel. This false gospel is not one that encourages holy and righteous living, which involves leading a witnessing lifestyle with Christ-like attitude daily, to the annoyance of the devil and those who hate the truth! Given the current state of the Church, the Lord Jesus has declared judgment against the worldly gospel, which promotes individual needs more than godly living. This false gospel also promotes the adoration and idolization of "servants of God." These preachers often preach a people-pleasing, motivational, prosperity-focused message. They avoid persecution by not speaking out against sinful conduct and encourage believers to embrace a worldly lifestyle of materialism.

Our Testimony is a Witness to Bible Message

In sharing this account on how this ministry started, we just wanted to share how the Lord Jesus established and commanded the activities of our Ministry. The Lord has also provided a global platform via a website (preparingforthekingdom.com) as a channel to reach our brothers and sisters far away with His Word and our testimony. This, He truthfully told us, is to prepare many people for His imminent return, which He promised us through many visions and messages, would occur in our lifetime. Our aim is therefore not to promote ourselves, but to share our testimony as a witness to what the Bible teaches and encourage you to be ready.

CHAPTER 2

God, Our Heavenly Father

...The Lord, the Lord God, merciful and gracious, longsuffering, and abounding in goodness and truth... (Exodus 34:6 NKJV)

The Lord has given us various subjects of Biblical foundation to write about, all centered on encouraging us to have a close relationship with Him. This message is a brief account about God, and we won't even be scratching the surface because He is infinite, great and beyond our understanding (Job 36:26). With the current environment in the world where there is an increase in violence, economic hardships, and natural disasters, people are turning to God – some for solace and comfort, and others for blame. Surely these types of events lead us to timeless questions about God, and the spiritually discerning will turn to 'sources' that give understanding about God.

As we know, some people around the world (even those who claim to be atheist or agnostic) have invented gods or idols that come in various forms and shapes, including material things and personal possessions. We Christians, on the other hand, believe in a Personal God who revealed Himself through nature (both in the terrestrial and in the celestial realms) and the Holy Bible (Romans 1:19-20; Genesis 1:27; 1 Samuel 3:21). The Bible makes no attempt to prove to us the existence of God; it asserts His existence from the beginning (Genesis 1:1; John 1:1-3). This God is neither an impersonal 'force' nor an abstract 'principle'; He is a Living Being, and people find the true meaning of His existence by coming into an active relationship with Him (John 17:3). In a vision, the Lord Jesus said to us, *"The message about GOD is very, very, very IMPORTANT. GOD is our GOOD NEWS!"*

Personal God

In order to understand God, as Christians our primary source should be His revealed truth—the Bible—which illuminates His character and Person more fully. This same God has also given us a spirit of faith to help us understand who He is and what He expects of us (Romans 12:3). Although Moses knew about the God of his fathers prior to fleeing from Egypt (Hebrews 11:24-26), he had his first personal encounter with God at the burning bush at the age of eighty (Exodus 3:1-4). Paul too had a personal encounter with God (Acts 9:1-6), and so did the rest of the Lord's disciples (John 21:25). Their encounters with the Living Christ gave them a personal faith to trust and obey His teachings. Even without a dramatic encounter with God, He has provided us with faith (Ephesians 2:8-9; Romans 12:3) and revelation about Himself so that we may know who He is and obey Him (John 20:29,31).

Having received the revelation of God by faith, *"...we also believe and therefore speak"* (2 Corinthians 4:13 NIV), we do not try to "prove" or argue whether God exists or not. As we reflect upon our awareness of right and wrong, we may also conclude that there is a moral God to whom all rational creatures are to be answerable to (Acts 17:23; Romans 2:15-16). Indeed, God has revealed Himself more fully through history, and that revelation is recorded in the Bible (Jeremiah 1:1-3; 1 Peter 1:21). The central truth of this revelation is that there is One God (Deuteronomy 6:4; Isaiah 44:6; Jeremiah

10:10), who exists in the form of Trinity (Genesis 1:1-3; Job 33:4; Psalm 33:6; John 1:1-4; John 16:13-15).

When we undertake any study on the character of God, we must bear in mind that God is a unified personality. He is not made up of many parts. He does not simply have certain qualities like goodness, truth, love, holiness and wisdom; He is the full expression of these qualities. The Bible portrays God more fully in this way: He is love, He is light, and He is the way, the truth, and the life (John 14:6; 1 John 1:5; 4:16).

God is Eternal and Totally Independent

God created man in His image (Genesis 1:26-27), and we are dependent on Him for breath (Job 33:4; Isaiah 42:5) and food (Genesis 1:29-30). However, God is not dependent on man or anything (Acts 17:24-28). Throughout history and more so today, many people have, under the inspiration of the devil, tried to disprove the existence of God (Psalm 14:1). They have used every form of blasphemy and argument to try and discourage those faithful believers whom God has revealed Himself to, but to no avail. Today, God is still being preached and obeyed throughout the world. Soon, we will see His Righteous Judgement upon those who mock Him and don't take Him seriously (Romans 2:15-16; Acts 17:29-31). Many don't believe because they think they will be able to escape giving account for their sins. This is Satan's trap to let them enjoy the temporary pleasures of sin while being blinded and corrupted by their "knowledge". For atheists or agnostics who simply don't believe that God exists, their unbelief holds no hope or future reward; they want to see in order to believe, but this is not a life based on faith (John 20:26-29).

Due to our human limitations, it is impossible to give a complete definition of God and the Bible forbids the use of anything in nature or anything made by man as a physical image of God (Exodus 20:4-5; Deuteronomy 4:15-19). When Moses asked for God's name so that he could share with the children of Israel some idea of His character, God revealed the name "I AM WHO I AM" (Exodus 3:14). God's response was to tell the people that He was independent, eternal and unchangeable.

God's existence cannot be measured in time, for He is without beginning and without end (Psalm 90:2; Isaiah 48:12; John 5:26; Romans 1:23). His Wisdom is immeasurable and therefore beyond the full understanding of man (Psalm 147:5; Isaiah 40:28; Daniel 2:20). God is infinite and without needs; absolutely nothing in creation or in activities of humans or angels can add anything to Him or take anything from Him (Psalm 50:10-13; Acts 17:24-25; Romans 11:36). He is not under anyone's obligation and He depends on no one. Whatever He does, He does because He chooses to, not because He is required to (Ephesians 1:11).

When the Lord gave us messages and visions about pastors and others, many people said we are "judging", but that is not true. It is the Lord who exposed the wickedness of those brethren and He gave the messages to correct and lead them to repentance. As members of the body of Christ, we have been granted the grace to speak God's message to the believers on His behalf, *"For the time has come for judgment to begin at the house of God; and if it begins with us first, what will be the end of those who do not obey the gospel of God?" (1 Peter 4:17 NKJV).*

God is Majestic and Sovereign

God is the absolute Good News to those who fear and obey Him. As Creator and Ruler of all things, He is enthroned in majesty in the Heavens above (Psalm 47:7; 93:1-2; 95:3-5; Hebrews 1:3; Isaiah 6:1-3). God is the possessor of absolute authority and nothing can exist independent of it (Psalm 2:1-6; Isaiah 2:10-12, 20-22; 40:23). He maintains the whole creation (Psalm 147:8-9; Matthew 5:45; Colossians 1:17). God has absolute knowledge and Presence. This is a cause for both our fear and joy. We say fear because no sin can escape Him, and joy because those who trust in His mercy will never be disappointed (Psalm 139:1-12; Proverbs 15:3; Isaiah 40:27-28; 57:15).

In conclusion, since God is sovereign, all people must repent, submit to Him and obey Him (Acts 17:30-31). While the Lord has given us choice and free will, refusal to obey is rebelliousness against Him, and this has eternal consequences (Matthew 25:46; Romans 6:23; Revelation 20:15; 21:8). When we try to be independent of God, we automatically become slaves to sin (Genesis 3:1-7; John 8:34). Unless we repent of our rebellious ways and surrender fully before our Sovereign God, trusting solely in His grace and forgiveness, there is no other way to escape God's wrath and judgment (Acts 17:30-31; Ephesians 2:8).

Finally, don't allow anyone to hinder your faith and walk with God. If you keep seeking the Lord, praying faithfully every day, studying the Bible, obeying His commands, living holy and repenting of your sins, your salvation and victory will be sure in Christ Jesus.

A Visit to Heaven

Vision given to Charis on May 16, 2011

This was the vision the Lord showed me. I saw the Lord coming down on a pure white cloud and He said: *"Come, My daughter Charis. Come and hold My hand."* I found myself riding on a cloud and we went high in the sky. The next moment we were in Heaven and I saw very beautiful and different colored flowers; flowers and colors I had never seen on earth. These were on each side of the golden shiny road; I did not see or feel any dust whatsoever.

We then arrived at a very long table, the Lord's Table that had no ending. I saw a pure white sheet with a golden stripe in the middle. There were golden cups, plates, and cutlery everything seemed ready to be used. We just glanced at the table and what was upon it. Shortly afterward I felt like we went through another door and I saw the Big Father sitting high up. I lifted my head to look at Him, but His face was all brilliant light so I could not see His eyes. However, from His chest down, I noticed a golden sash with these words written on it: "*I Am The Father*". I then saw the Lord Jesus Christ's throne to the right of the Big Father. It had very beautiful precious stones of different kinds. While standing before the Throne of God, I could see afar off some Angels who were busy performing activities, but I could not tell what they were doing.

The Big Father spoke to me and said: *"Don't be scared, My daughter Charis. I just love you very, very, very, very, very much."* After the Father spoke these Words to me, and with my hand still in the Lord's hand, we came down from Heaven and I found myself at home in our backyard, where the Lord always meets with me. He told me that He loved me and my family. The Lord then said He was coming again on Wednesday (His next visit).

CHAPTER 3

Have Faith in God

But without faith it is impossible to please Him, for he who comes to God must believe that He is, and that He is a rewarder of those who diligently seek Him (Hebrews 11:6 NKJV).

The Bible tells us that having faith, that is, believing and trusting God without any reservations, is an important prerequisite to receiving from God. We are also reminded that as we believe, so it shall be:

He touched their eyes, saying, "According to your faith let it be to you" (Matthew 9:29 NKJV).

And whatever things you ask in prayer, believing, you will receive" (Matthew 21:22 NKJV).

On the other hand, expressing doubt in God, I AM THAT I AM (Exodus 3:14), and not believing that with Him all things are possible (Matthew 19:26), amounts to lacking faith and no results can be expected! Whether to have faith or doubt is a choice; however, faith is pleasing to God (Hebrews 11:6).

Some Christians might think that they don't need this message because they believe that they already have faith. My fellow brethren, we all need this message, because no amount of faith is going to be enough (Luke 17:5). We should keep growing in our faith! The Lord said that as diverse as the various members of the body are for the good of the whole body, the gifts are likewise diversified for our edification and maturity in our faith (1 Corinthians 12:4-5; Ephesians 4:11-13). We therefore highly recommend that you read the quoted Scriptures in all our articles, always!

There are diversities of gifts, but the same Spirit. There are differences of ministries, but the same Lord (1 Corinthians 12:4-5 NKJV).

And He Himself gave some to be apostles, some prophets, some evangelists, and some pastors and teachers, for the equipping of the saints for the work of ministry, for the edifying of the body of Christ, till we all come to the unity of the faith and of the knowledge of the Son of God, to a perfect man, to the measure of the stature of the fullness of Christ... (Ephesians 4:11-13 NKJV).

Having faith in God involves acquiring the knowledge to trust and love Someone who has supreme abilities to guard us against our fears and insecurities. We have hope when we accept the unseen reality of a Supreme Being, even when we are faced with uncertainties (Romans 10:17; Hebrews 11:1). It is indeed true that the message about faith is ancient, going as far back as the first generation of our forefathers (Hebrews 11:4). However, today many people still fail the test of faith. True faith is not just about confessing and believing in a Supreme Being. Such faith is casual and hopelessly fruitless because it is not based on a relationship and merits no change in our character. In other words, simply believing in God, without depth and commitment, is not enough; even the demons believe—and tremble with terror and trepidation! (James 2:19).

As it is, there is no reward for having passive or inactive faith that lacks a committed relationship (Hebrews 11:6). Furthermore, it must be noted that this kind of faith is equivalent to atheism because an atheist says: "I do not believe in the existence of a God, so I am not going to do anything He requires from me!" A person with such an attitude is self-seeking and lost; they serve themselves and their works as their god. At best, they hope that there is no God so that they are not accountable for their lack of faith and unbelief, as well as their actions. Having discounted believing in the existence of a Supreme Being, their hope turns into vanity. Faith connects us to a relationship, commitment, and responsibility to God (James 2:14-26), for the Bible also clearly says that without faith it is impossible to please God. If you come to God, you must believe that He exists and that He rewards those who diligently seek Him (Hebrews 11:6).

To have a glimpse of how God rewards those who have faith, let us consider Joseph's experience in Egypt (Genesis 41). When Joseph interpreted the Pharaoh's dream, the pagan king acted by faith and set Joseph in charge over all the land of Egypt (Genesis 41:37-41). This act of faith saved his nation and other nations from severe famine (Genesis 41:53-57). Today, we still have many people who don't believe the word of God, and this will eventually lead to their own destruction unless they repent (Ezekiel 18:23; 33:11).

People outside the Christian faith perform certain rituals and ceremonies and follow rules to show commitment and faith to their gods. In Christ, however, we commit and obey God through voluntary love (John 14:23). No person born of God through the Holy Spirit finds His will burdensome if the love for the Lord controls them (Matthew 11:30). Those without love for the Lord find His will burdensome, and such faith is fruitless and dead (1 John 5:2-5).

Faith for Salvation

Undoubtedly, the Bible says that faith comes by hearing the Word of God (Romans 10:17). When we hear the Word of God, conviction from the Holy Spirit brings godly sorrow and repentance, and God grants us grace to accept His gift of faith and forgiveness (Ephesians 2:8; 2 Corinthians 7:10). From these and other

Scriptures, we see that no one inherits faith automatically (Jeremiah 31:30; Ezekiel 18:20; Galatians 6:5). God works in us as He places a 'witness' of His existence (His Holy Spirit) in our hearts and we accept by acknowledging His Supremacy (Romans 3:23).

Having accepted faith leading to our salvation, we are required to wait for our redemption and exercise (work on) our faith, proving God is in us by our transformed ways (Romans 12:2; John 15:8; 2 Corinthians 5:17; 1 John 3:9) and renewed inner intentions (Colossians 3:10).

Faith for Ministry

When we are called by God to do ministry work, He calls each one of us and anoints us according to the work needed to execute the duties He assigned to us (Exodus 31:1-6; Leviticus 8:12; John 1:32; Acts 13:2). Many believers have written to us asking how they can recognize the call of God upon their lives. Others even asked that we inquire from the Lord on their behalf and ask Him about their ministry calling. Because of their lack of faith, some people that we inquired for from the Lord did not even realize that the work they were presently doing in the body was from Him! In reply to them, the Lord chastened them for their lack of discernment. From their responses, we perceived that some of these believers thought that the Lord would say that He called them to be prophets or evangelists, thinking only of the official ministry offices. No ministry activity in the body of Christ is inferior to the other ministry gifts (1 Corinthians 12:21). The Lord designed the various gifts to serve one purpose, and that is to *"equip his people for works of service, so that the body of Christ may be built up until we all reach unity in the faith and in the knowledge of the Son of God and become mature, attaining to the whole measure of the fullness of Christ"* (Ephesians 4:12-13). Furthermore, in a message of encouragement from the Lord to some brethren who are doing street evangelism, He encouraged them to continue doing the work for His sake (Luke 9:50; 12:34).

There are brethren who are waiting for the 'formal' anointing by the laying on of hands by their leaders before they accept and acknowledge the calling of God in their lives. They will not do ministry work unless they are acknowledged or 'ordained' and 'blessed' by some church leader. This kind of conduct gives the impression that there is no conviction from the Holy Spirit, and that we should only accept ministry position from a church leader. From the Bible, however, we see that God does the calling (1 Samuel 3:4), and when He calls, He also anoints us for the task of our calling (Galatians 1:11-12). When the Lord calls us, there is a fresh tone and urgency in His message (Jeremiah 1:4-8). Admittedly, the laying on of hands for ministry service is a genuine Biblical practice. However, the one anointing is not the pastor or the person ordaining us, but The Lord Himself (Acts 13:2). In the Bible, we have examples of lay believers in Christ who went out preaching the gospel, healing the sick and driving out demons (Luke 9:50; Acts 8:4). Let us therefore not limit the Lord by thinking that only a few "special" or specific people are anointed or ordained for ministry work. The truth is that all believers are called to serve the Lord, but only those who express willingness to endure the work of the cross and are obedient to the Lord will be victorious (Matthew 22:14; Luke 10:1-3; 17-20).

Faith for Deliverance and Provision

In our ministry, we have had a few people who were unemployed, sick, and struggling with certain personal habits. The Lord told them to have faith and to fast if they needed to have breakthrough and deliverance. True to His word, some have experienced healing from various sicknesses, deliverance from sinful habits and demons, and the jobless ones who had enduring faith found employment. The key to victory was that their faith rested in the love for the Lord, and so they endured in obedience. As a result, they joyfully received God's promises. When we delight in the Lord and our motives are pure, pleasing to Him, and motivated by our submission to His ability and Supremacy over all things, God approves our faith in granting our requests (Psalm 37:4; Matthew 7:11; John 15:7).

Faith is a Choice

Biblically, faith is a choice or an option we should exercise daily. At every intersection in life's journey or in whatever circumstances we may face, we have the choice to either have faith and obey God's Word and commands or disregard them altogether (Joshua 24:15; Romans 6:16). When we have committed faith in the Lord, we *choose* to disregard the opinions of others and instead concentrate on our obedience to Him (Daniel 6:10).

You all might be aware of certain religions, sects or even "Christian" denominations that use fear as a weapon to force or coerce their followers to submit and act in a certain way. As a believer and follower of The Lord Jesus Christ, I have learned first-hand from our experiences with Him, that He never forces His will upon us (Revelation 3:20). Forced obedience does not emanate from faith and love, but from fear.

Let me share with you an experience I had with the Lord on choosing to have faith. A few months after the Lord showed my daughter Charis that a man closely related to my wife was in hell (we have shared this vision on our website, titled as "Visit to Hell"), the Lord in His unfailing mercy heard the pleas of his family and He sent me to go and preach the gospel to them. This was something I desired to do after learning of the man's eternal fate. The day before going to preach to the man's family, I had a very frustrating day at work, and I was so upset to the point that I asked the Lord in prayer to release me from going to preach at the family's residence. To my amazement, the Lord did not rebuke me for refusing to go where He had sent me. Instead, and to my wife's surprise, He gently gave my wife a message to go and preach to the family. After the Lord did this, I was overcome with guilt and shame for being disobedient to the Lord. I immediately repented and told my wife that I would go and preach to that family. Since the message that I was going to preach was very important, the Lord caused many people to attend the meeting. That evening, I delivered a powerful message and the Lord later commented, saying: *"Your father preached with the fire of the Holy Spirit!"*

Praise be to God who gives us His Spirit without limit *(John 3:34)*, to delight in Him and fear Him! *(Isaiah 11:2-3)*. Let us continue to explore further what it means to fear the Lord.

CHAPTER 4

Fearing God

And do not be drunk with wine, in which is dissipation; but be filled with the Spirit, speaking to one another in psalms and hymns and spiritual songs, singing and making melody in your heart to the Lord, giving thanks always for all things to God the Father in the name of our Lord Jesus Christ, submitting to one another in the fear of God (Ephesians 5:18-21 NKJV)

A simple search of the online Bible reveals that the word "fear" is used well over 100 times in reference to God. The Bible admonishes us not only to honor all people (including our leaders) and love our brothers and sisters in Christ, but to fear and honor the Lord as well (1 Peter 2:17 NKJV). Furthermore, the Word of God also teaches us that fearing God is required for one to gain wisdom (Proverbs 1:7; 9:10; 15:33; Psalm 111:10).

Initially, when we fear God, we spontaneously and submissively yield to His will in humble reverence and awe to His authority. The single best freedom humanity can enjoy for all time is Truth! Why? Because Truth sets us free (John 8:32)—no guilt, worry, fear, possessions, or fleshly desires are attached to truth. That Truth is Jesus Christ, and it is only through Him that we can have true freedom and eternal life (John 8:36; 14:6).

Naturally, when we correct our children (who have been taught in the ways of the Lord) after they have misbehaved, their response to our rebuke is often with reverence and with a sense of fear for God. As our Lord said, children are humble and more responsive to the fear of God than adults (Matthew 18:3-4). The Lord's promise to us, as parents, is that if we bring up our children in the ways of the Lord, we would reap the benefit of them walking in the fear of God all the days of their lives (1 Samuel 1:21-28; Proverbs 22:6).

How We Lose our Fear of God

From the Bible, we learn that the fear of God is the foundation to attaining wisdom (Proverbs 1:7; 9:10; 15:33; Psalm 111:10). Alluding to this fact, the Word of God warns us to guard against and avoid "godless chatter" or "profane and idle babblings and contradictions" or "irreverent empty speeches" that the world considers to be "knowledge" or "staying informed"; these types of talks and arguments will surely dilute and deviate our faith (1 Timothy 6:20-21). In my experience, and from what I have observed, we indeed start losing our fear for God when we are drawn to other interests which direct us away from God. Some of these distractions are well explained in the Bible; for example worldliness, love of money, and addictions (1 John 2:15; James 4:4; 2 Corinthians 6:14). In addition to these, I have identified a few other influences that also contribute negatively to our relationship with God.

Desires: To us Christians, the Bible is God's infallible Word which carries a life-changing and life-giving instruction to mankind. We read in the Bible how several people, who knew God and had a relationship with Him initially, defied His will and chose to walk contrary to His ways (2 Chronicles 24:17-19; 2 Timothy 4:10). Exercising God's will is a choice, and defying sin brings us two victories: God's acceptance of our obedience and freedom from guilt. Our weakness as humans is that our choices are often influenced by our desires, which come either through someone or something that our senses capture. For example, Adam and Eve gave into the devil's temptation when Eve *"saw that the fruit of the tree was good for food and pleasing to the eye, and also desirable for gaining wisdom...."*(Genesis 3:1-6). Likewise, David gave in to lust and committed adultery when he saw that *"...the woman was very beautiful..."* (2 Samuel 11:1-4).

Influence from others: Bad influence from others can also detract our choice for obedience (1 Corinthians 15:33). For example, two arrogant men, Azariah and Johanan, falsely accused the Prophet Jeremiah of lying, and they influenced the people to flee to Egypt, contrary to God's warning (Jeremiah 43:1-7). Also, in the Garden of Eden, the serpent influenced Eve to sin, and in turn Eve influenced Adam (Genesis 3:6). Rehoboam, who succeeded his father Solomon as king over Israel, was influenced by the young men he had grown up with to impose greater burdens on the people. He rejected the wise counsel of the elders who had urged him to be a servant leader and serve his people with equity and kindness (1 Kings 12:1–15).

Fear of man: Many people often fall into the trap of rejecting Godly counsel in exchange for human counsel and sympathy; this is giving victory to the devil. In the Scriptures, such an attitude is best described by these words from King Saul: *"I have sinned. I violated the LORD's command and your instructions. I was afraid of the men and so I gave in to them"* (1 Samuel 15:24). During the time of Exodus, of the twelve men sent by Moses to spy the land of Canaan, only two (Caleb and Joshua) expressed confidence that God would help Israel conquer the land, and they urged the people not to have confidence in God and not rebel against Him, because the Lord was with them (Numbers 13:30; 14:6-9). The remaining ten spies were afraid and scared of "the giants", so they discouraged the people and influenced them to rebel against Moses and Aaron (Numbers 13:31-

33; 14:1-4, 10). The Hebrew midwives (Shiphrah and Puah) stood faithfully; they *"... feared God and did not do what the king of Egypt had told them to do; they let the boys live"* (Exodus 1:17). The prophet Daniel also, when he learned of the plot against him, was not afraid. Instead of giving in to fear, *"he knelt down on his knees three times that day, and prayed and gave thanks before his God, as was his custom since early days"* (Daniel 6:10 NKJV). The Bible warns us that *"fear of man will prove to be a snare, but whoever trusts in the LORD is kept safe"* (Proverbs 29:25). We should not fear man or seek to please others, but God alone (Isaiah 2:22; Isaiah 51:12; Galatians 1:10; 1 Thessalonians 2:4; Colossians 3:23; 2 Corinthians 5:9; 2 Timothy 1:7). Moreover, the Lord Jesus Christ Himself reiterated that we should *"not fear those who kill the body but cannot kill the soul. But rather fear Him who is able to destroy both soul and body in hell"* (Matthew 10:28).

Possessions and power: Today's economic environment is quite enticing to many. The explosion of goods, services, and flashy new technologies in the market makes it very easy for the devil to tempt us. Consequently, material things and thirst for power can separate us from God's will (Matthew 19:16-23; Luke 8:14). There are some wealthy and influential people in this world whose power is their possessions and they have no fear of God. In their lust and greed for more material things, they reject eternal life—the most precious of all gifts—for worldly gain and the short-lived pleasure of sin (Luke 12:13-21; Hebrews 11:25). Sadly, many people are following them.

As a fact, today's booming worldly entertainment media, such as television, movies, the Internet, videos and social media, promote the breakdown of family relationships and have become great stumbling blocks to godly living. In personal messages to many of us, the Lord admonished and encouraged us not to fear men. Although we are commanded to respect all men (1 Peter 2:17), we must not be afraid of their opinions of us, nor should we be ashamed of our convictions and our faith in the Lord Jesus Christ (Acts 5:26-32).

Are You Living for God or for Your Own Pleasures?

Not too long ago, the Lord spoke to us in a vision, saying that we are hated by many Christians because of sharing His strong messages of rebuke against sin and wicked practices in the Church (John 17:14). We love doing the Lord's work and our fear is for the Lord God alone. The Lord's message is a strong warning against worldliness among Christians (Matthew 13:18-22; Romans 8:7).

As a ministry, the value we attach to truthful living and holiness far exceeds the luxuries of this life. While some may boast about their [temporary] power and earthly possessions, we know they are also driven by guilt and a strong fear of death. We should not value useless things above God and allow others to sway us from the path of truth; even in caring for others we must seek to please God (Matthew 7:13-14; 13:18-23). In the Book of Acts, we read about how Ananias and his wife Sapphira lost their lives as a result of greed for money and love of worldly possessions (Acts 5:1-11); what they treasured controlled them (Matthew 6:21). Using their example as a warning, we should not exchange the fear of God for anything; be it riches, power, or fame (Matthew 16:26). Instead, we should strive to faithfully and obediently serve God and allow nothing to separate us from Him (Romans 8:38-39). Like Job, we are encouraged to be wise by fearing the Lord and shunning evil (Job 1:1; 2:3; Proverbs 14:16; Ecclesiastes 12:13).

There are many Christian leaders who encourage us to "follow your heart" and "pursue your dreams." The question we should ask ourselves is this: how do those dreams and plans in our hearts measure up to God's will? Are those dreams only in pursuit of worldly happiness, comfort, and "success", without the Cross of Jesus? If so, as the Lord Jesus explained in the Parable of the Rich Fool (Luke 12:16-21), your dreams are self-serving and for your own glory, and they will only inspire those who seek praise from man! In contrast, pursuing godly dreams through the cross of Jesus, despite persecution and hatred from the world, will lead to the salvation of others, resulting in glory to Christ. The Bible teaches us that Truth through the cross comes at the cost of insults, hatred and blood (Luke 6:22; John 15:18; 2 Timothy 3:12; 1 Peter 3:16; 4:12-14; 2 Corinthians 4:8-12). Do you think any of Christ' followers conquered the world being applauded by the masses, without insults and hatred from the world which hates the truth? (Matthew 5:11; John 15:18).

Are you struggling with sins or temptations, be they thoughts, habits, addictions, or behaviors that drive you from the fear of God? Repent and conquer them in Jesus' name, for the power is in your possession — choice (Genesis 4:6-7) and the Lord is willing to set you free (Acts 2:38; 3:19; 8:22; 1 John 1:9; Romans 6:6-7). Is the fear of man and of persecution holding you back from fearing God, serving Him, and doing His will? The Lord Jesus can set you free if you receive Him into your heart and follow Him as your Master, Lord, and Savior (John 8:32; 36). I, therefore, urge you to *"...fear the Lord, serve Him in sincerity and in truth, and put away the gods... Serve the Lord! And if it seems evil to you to serve the Lord, choose for yourselves this day whom you will serve... But as for me and my house, we will serve the Lord"* (Joshua 24:14-15 NKJV).

The Addiction and Idolatry of Watching Television

Vision given to Charis on May 13, 2014

In a vision to Charis, the Lord showed her three yellow images in the sky: a smiling face with one tick mark, a sad face with three tick marks, and an angry face with two tick marks. This is what The Lord said they represent:

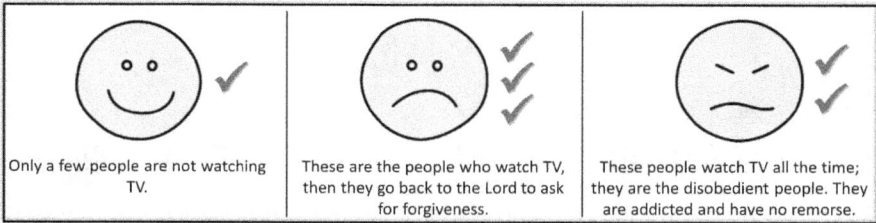

Only a few people are not watching TV.	These are the people who watch TV, then they go back to the Lord to ask for forgiveness.	These people watch TV all the time; they are the disobedient people. They are addicted and have no remorse.

- **The smiling face:** Of the entire Christians worldwide, only a few are not watching secular television, and the Lord is very pleased with those Christians.
- **The sad face:** These are Christians who watch secular television, then they go back to the Lord and ask for forgiveness, repeating the same thing. This makes the Lord very sad!
- **The angry face:** These are the people who are watching secular television all the time. They are the disobedient Christians who are addicted to television and show no remorse. The Lord is angry with those who practice such disobedience.

Note: A good Christian TV channel preaching the Word of God is acceptable. However, sitting in front of the contraption daily leads to addiction and encourages laziness. It is, therefore, better to choose Bible reading and prayer instead of watching TV. When watching TV, always be led by the Holy Spirit and set limits.

CHAPTER 5

Why Do You Put Your Shoes On Wrong Feet?

On Saturday, January 14, 2012, the Lord showed Charis a Vision of all the people in the world standing on a giant platform and looking at a preacher of the Gospel. Among those present were Christians as well as non-believers—everyone in the world, including you. The man she identified as a preacher looked at all the people standing before him and asked them, "People, why do you put your shoes on the wrong feet? You have been living disobediently to God!" As the preacher asked that question, Charis noticed that all people had their shoes swapped around. The people responded in unison: "Oh, we have forgotten to put on our shoes correctly!" In a cursive writing, these words then appeared in the sky: *"People are turning away from the Lord"*.

When we asked the Lord about this vision, He said that many people have turned away from the true Gospel and they are following their own direction. Even those who claim to be born-again are walking in disobedience and this is grieving the Lord. In a message to this ministry and the Church at large, the Lord commanded us to *Preach the Gospel and the Power of Salvation through the Cross, avoid godless quarrels, and encourage Holy living.* As a member of the body of Christ, brethren, the Lord is calling you to walk in the spirit of Stephen and Phillip, to lead a witnessing lifestyle. Now, what or who is holding you back? Are you ashamed of sharing the Gospel at the expense of souls getting lost?

Let me share a brief testimony as an encouragement to you to share the Gospel. Before the Lord called and established this ministry, I was out in the streets witnessing with gospel tracts that I had ordered from Fellowship Tract League. I have had a very positive experience with this organization, and I have enjoyed a long and fruitful relationship with the people there. I also have found them to be very useful in helping individual Christians who would like to make a positive impact in people's lives with the Gospel. If you are ready to start witnessing and are interested in ordering gospel tracts, I strongly encourage you to contact this organization. The Lord forbid that we use our work, sickness, age or family as an excuse not to witness! We had a brother who witnessed with us in the past, and in a strong message, the Lord rebuked him for using excuses not to witness. The Lord said: *"My son [John] does not care about Me."* Subsequently, the brother obeyed and never skipped witnessing. Let us, therefore, prepare the world for the Lord's soon return by being diligent in witnessing!

Vision of Christians Backsliding (Apostasy)

Now brethren, this is a very important vision that we are sharing below. After the Lord started speaking to Charis in January 2010, He showed her this same vision about four times a week. She would share it with me, but I just ignored it, until the Lord alerted me that message pertaining to vision was important to share with the world. We are therefore sharing this vision not only to encourage you to witness, but also to remain faithful to your faith and salvation. This is what my daughter Charis shared:

"Every second night, the Lord shows me (without saying anything to me) a huge black figure (I am made aware in the vision that this is the devil) made out of smoke or steam in the shape of a man standing on the

left side of a shiny golden street, and a huge White and Light-emitting
Figure (I know this is the Lord) on the right side of the golden street.
Both these figures have people standing behind them that reflect their
color or texture. In the vision, I could sense that after about every 15
minutes or so, three to four people would leave the side of White Figure
and go to the side of the black figure. The moment these people left the
White figure to go to the other side of the street, they became black from
their feet up and stood behind the black figure. This black figure would
then lift up his head and laugh; while I could not see his face, I could see
his long yellow teeth as he was laughing.

On the other hand, I was able to feel that the White figure is not
happy but sad when people leave and cross to the side of the devil, the
black figure. After waiting for a very long time, almost an hour in time
measurement, I would see just one person leaving the black figure and
going over to the White Figure. When this happened, I could feel the joy
and excitement of the White Figure while the black figure became very
angry at his loss. However, soon after this one person joined the Lord's
side, I would see three or four people leaving the Lord's side and go over
to the laughing black figure. Although the Lord was saying nothing
while this scene played out, I knew in my heart that He was hurt when
people turned away from Him to go back to the world and the devil."

Just when we thought this vision was over, on November 5, 2012,
the Lord added to this vision. He added "The Bullies", represented
by a yellow color—those who intimidate the truly faithful and God-
fearing. Two days later (on November 7, 2012), the Lord added "The
Humble People," who were represented by a purple color. Below are
the meanings and interpretation of this vision.

Meaning of the Vision of Christians Back-sliding (Apostasy):

On the night of November 25, 2012, the Lord Jesus Christ unveiled the meaning of the vision of the black figure, the White Figure, and the other two new scenes He added, as Charis explains below.

The White Side (Faithful Witness)

"On the above night, the Lord again showed me this vision. This time, I was allowed to see the face of one person who is part of our ministry team, and it was my father. The Lord only allowed me to see my father's face, but not the rest of the other brethren standing there with the Lord. Their faces were dazzling white but blurred, so I could not recognize them. My father was standing there reading his Bible, and after reading, he closed it and started speaking. However, I could not hear what he was saying, but the Lord looked at him intently. I heard the voice of the Lord saying: "Look at My son; he is very obedient. He is reading his Bible faithfully every day, and he is praying faithfully daily. He is a faithful witness of My Word. I am going to bless him abundantly" (Matthew 25:21; Revelation 3:4-6). Soon after saying this, the Lord made me understand that this is the inheritance of the faithful and obedient Christians; they will be rewarded with His Presence forever for being obedient. I was shown a beautiful scene playing out right before me on how the people on the White Side were going about their work and the good they inherited. However, the Lord did not allow me to remember the exact detail, but only what I am sharing here. After the Lord showed me the various activities happening on the White side I turned to my right and saw another group of people. All the people standing there were covered in a purple color.

The Purple Side (Humble People)

Just right above this group of people was a board written in pink cursive letters, "The humble people". Like on the White side, the people on this side were covered in a rich, purple color to disguise their faces. The Lord did, however, show me a face of a person and she was one of our ministry members. The Lord looked at her and said: "Look at My daughter; she is very humble and she allows nothing to discourage her. I am also going to bless her abundantly" (Matthew 5:5; Revelation 2:25-26). Thereafter I was shown another group of people further away.

The Yellow Side (Bullies)

There was also a board in yellow cursive writing above this group that read: "The Bullies". These people were covered in a yellow substance and again I was allowed only to see the face of only one person, who is both a mother and grandmother.

This person belongs to this group and being a lukewarm Christian, she is the religious type. These are those who live off every word of their leaders. They are responsible for using their religious knowledge to cause others to stumble. They encourage disobedience and lukewarm living, like wild partying and engaging in the watching of worldly television and movies. These people are literally addicted to worldly things, but they would never skip their Saturday or Sunday Church service. Brethren, this is the harlot (Revelation 17:1). Like I said above, this is the territory of the unfaithful, lukewarm and disobedient Christians. These types of Christians prostitute themselves with the teachings of other religions. They despise the Holy Word of God and He has decreed Judgement on them. The Lord showed Charis the activity of this woman. While most of it is symbolic, the point the Lord is making is that this group is completely wicked. They show no regard for God and His Word. They are worldly, and they follow after worldly gain and wealth while they display a despising attitude towards those who are less fortunate. Charis continues to share the vision from the Lord:

"I saw this elderly woman standing next to an old black radio. The radio was on and I heard people talking very loudly from a secular station. As a

habit, this woman had her radio on almost all day listening to various talk shows and music. I noticed that she had a Bible in her right hand, and as I was looking, she suddenly threw the Bible violently to the floor and started jumping on it several times. I saw her pick up the Book of Mormon, which was lying on a small table next to her, and she started reading from it. Soon after reading the Mormon book, she put it down gently and picked up a Quran and also started reading it. To my surprise, she picked up the Bible from the floor, but not to read it. She started tearing some pages from the Bible and put them in her mouth and spit them on the floor. I then saw her holding the Bible with both her hands and shaking it violently as if she was saying, "I hate you!" Just then I heard the voice of the Lord saying: "Look at her; she is making My Holy Word a doormat. She is despising My Word, and she is reading things that she is not supposed to read. I am going to punish her severely" (Revelation 18). Soon after this revelation, I was made to turn to the black figure and his group of people."

In understanding the meaning of this vision, the Lord is saying there are many Christians who are despising His Word and His teachings. These Christians are more interested in the "tickle the ear" teachings of other religions, false teachers, and various motivational speakers and talk shows on radio and television, instead of fully following Biblical truth (2 Timothy 4:3-4). Meanwhile, the Bible has everything we need to know and to live by (2 Timothy 3:16).

The Black Figure (World of Pleasure)

"When I looked at this group of people, I was again allowed to look at the face of one person whom I also knew very well. I heard the Lord say: "Look at that one, he is drinking and smoking, partying and he is all over the place (I could see him moving from one place to another on the black side; he appeared completely restless, a busy-body). I am also going to punish him severely" (Revelation 21:8). I also saw this man holding a glass of whiskey and ice with a long cigar in his mouth. His eyes were blood-shot.

People seemed to just move around unrestrained while the devil was standing there laughing as if saying "keep partying, dancing and enjoying yourselves!" After the Lord showed me this vision, He showed me a vision involving a pastor who was judged for listening to and encouraging worldly music.

Below is an illustration of the vision of the four sides.

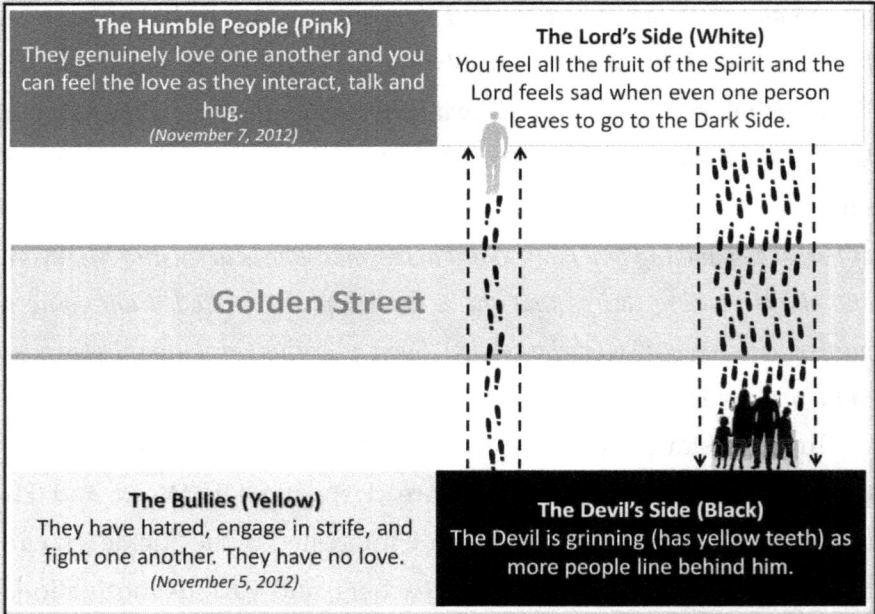

The Humble People (Pink)	The Lord's Side (White)
They genuinely love one another and you can feel the love as they interact, talk and hug. *(November 7, 2012)*	You feel all the fruit of the Spirit and the Lord feels sad when even one person leaves to go to the Dark Side.

Golden Street

The Bullies (Yellow)	The Devil's Side (Black)
They have hatred, engage in strife, and fight one another. They have no love. *(November 5, 2012)*	The Devil is grinning (has yellow teeth) as more people line behind him.

In concluding this vision, I beseech you brethren, please remain faithful to the Lord, and persevere in obedience every moment of your life. Hold on to your salvation as it is worth eternal life. While waiting for the Lord to appear, labor in His harvest field, witness to obtain Heavenly wealth (Matthew 24:45-47).

CHAPTER 6

Duties of a True Born-again Christian

The Lord has given us this message to encourage and remind us of our duties as Christians. Being our Master and Lord, the Lord Jesus requires all Christians to obey and submit to Him (John 14:23; James 4:7). Please don't be tired if we keep repeating or emphasizing some points; this is for your benefit (Philippians 3:1). The duties we will consider here are by no means exhaustive as revealed in the Scriptures. For practical purposes, we will consider the most basic Christian duties, especially in the light of what the Lord has repeatedly revealed to us as a family and ministry. As born-again Christians, we must live to care about the things the Lord cares about, thus doing good deeds in obedience to God (James 2:14-17).

Being Born Again to Worship the Lord

From what we read in the Scriptures, the Lord expects every one of us who are truly born-again Christian to serve and follow Him faithfully every second of our existence (Matthew 25:4, 10). After we become born again and accept the gift of salvation, in God's eyes we became a new creation and we are told to *"take off the old man corrupted by evil desires"* (2 Corinthians 5:17; Ephesians 4:22-25). The 'old man', referring to our former way of living, was corrupted by worldliness and the desires onto which our carnal nature fed (Romans 12:1-2; Galatians 5:17-26). The first step towards reunification with God is to confess our sins and pledge obedience to Christ Jesus (Romans 10:9-10; 1 John 1:9). In doing this, we simply confess our faith in His redemptive work, acknowledging that we cannot be saved by any other means except through the Cross. In our allegiance to obedience, we declare that we will follow Him faithfully through the teachings of His word, no matter what obstacles we may face. In other words, we declare unity and co-existence with Him, like in a marital vow (1 Corinthians 6:17), whereby a husband and wife promised before God to remain together no matter what! We confess our sins to one another, forgive, and ask for forgiveness (Ephesians 4:32; 1 John 1:9; James 5:16).

As challenging as it is to maintain a solid marriage, we learn to grow in patience for the benefit of the other person; considering that when we do good, it is for our encouragement (Philippians 2:3). So then, when we allow our love for the other person in the marriage to control us, this experience will change us to the benefit of our spouse. In similar fashion, our love for Christ must compel us to obey and honor Him (2 Corinthians 5:14-15). We surrendered the "old self" and put on the 'new self', which is being created to be like God in true righteousness and holiness (Ephesians 4:22, 24; Colossians 3:10).

The Bible also encourages to worship the Lord (Exodus 23:25; John 4:24). Whether we meet as a group to fellowship together or when we do so alone, we are expected to worship our God and adore Him for the great and wondrous things He has done and for Who He Is (Psalm 66:1-20). Like David, our lifestyle must be one of worship and giving glory to our Heavenly Father (1 Thessalonians 5:18).

Obedience to Christ

The Bible warns us against sinning deliberately (Hebrews 10:26). We learned this first hand when the Lord, in a gesture of love, punished a sister in our ministry who was willfully sinning by smoking cigarettes in private and engaging in immorality. The Lord barred her from praying with the ministry intercessory team for five weeks and from witnessing with the team. She could attend normal services but was not allowed to do ministry work. People need to realize that the Lord does not allow people guilty of sexual sins to pray for others in the assembly of intercessors. The Lord is Holy! Another sister who committed a serious sexual sin was denied blessings. She was unrepentant after sinning and employment opportunities were closed for her. She lost her job and is still unemployed.

Please don't get me wrong: the Lord forgives us when we have done wrong. However, He is not pleased when we sin willfully; this is being disobedient (Hebrews 12:6). Love does not cause harm to others (Romans 13:10), so if we say that we love the Lord, we must act in obedience; this is our Christian duty (Ecclesiastes 12:13; John 14:15, 23).

Daily Bible Reading and Witnessing are Christian Duties

When we go to our various places of work every day, don't we show commitment and love for our work? Similarly, we show our commitment and love to God by obeying His commands, witnessing, Bible reading, praying, doing good to others, and abstaining from conforming to worldly standards (Mark 16:15; Joshua 1:8; Psalm 55:17; 1 Thessalonians 5:17; Romans 12:10; 12:1-2). During the Lord's first visitation to us, the first thing He commanded us to do was to read our Bibles every day and *"not to take a holiday away from the WORD OF GOD."* We were not in the habit of reading the Bible consistently, but read every other day or as we felt. Truly this kind of behavior does not reflect obedience to Scriptural command, nor does it show commitment to what is supposed to be our passion. I can tell you, the many people who got messages from the Lord through this ministry, almost all of them were commanded to build their relationship with God through reading their Bibles every day. In my experience, and having observed the behavior of my own family, our daily Bible reading did not just increase our knowledge about God and His works; we have also experienced a change in our attitudes and behaviors. This has also resulted in our faith increasing in the Lord, and our relationship with Him has grown closer (Romans 10:17). Consequently, this has led us to trust in Him completely, knowing that He hears and meets our various prayer requests (John 15:7). Furthermore, in addition to the above, another benefit of seeking God through prayer and Bible reading is that our fear for Him increases. This fear is one of appreciating His Authority as our Heavenly Father, and with this comes His many blessings, including the outpouring of His Spirit upon us. When we receive His Spirit, we also receive some Fruit of the Holy Spirit and gifts for ministry work (John 15:4-8).

Even though being corrected by others may embarrass us or cause us to become defensive, when we read the Word of God the precious Holy Spirit convicts us and creates a humble submission and appreciation of God's love for us. This ensures we have a peaceful relationship with Him based on love. To achieve this, the Lord encourages us to be wise men and women of God by not just being hearers only but also being doers of the Word (James 1:22; Matthew 7:24-27). Let us keep seeking the Lord so that like King David we may have a heart full of joy and appreciation to delight ourselves in the transforming power of the Holy Word of God (Psalm 19:7-11). To God alone through Christ Jesus be the Glory forever, Amen!

Our Duty to Pray Daily Expresses God's Sovereignty

While we briefly discussed the topic of prayer above, it is necessary to discuss further. The Apostle Paul admonishes us to *"...pray without ceasing..."* (1 Thessalonians 5:17). Brethren, let me be straight forward with you here: a Christian who does not pray is lukewarm, spiritually dead, and lazy; this is essentially expressing an attitude of "I don't need God". As it is, if we don't pray, we show no care about our own salvation, that of others, and neither do we operate in obedience to Christ (Philippians 2:21). Indeed, such an attitude clearly shows that we don't gather with Him, so neither do we intercede with Him to save and deliver others (Luke 11:23; Ezekiel 22:30).

In a further warning, the Lord warned His disciples to pray and be watchful (Luke 21:36). The Lord, having being in the world, knew the afflictions and sufferings that Satan can bring upon us (Isaiah 53:3-5), and the curse that God pronounced on the earth which does not work or our good (Genesis 3:17). He, therefore, encourages us to pray and set an example for us (Hebrews 5:7-10). When praying, we literally take stock of the conditions around us and in us and surrender these stressful situations to God to resolve so that it may go well with us (1 Timothy 2:2). Only God holds the answers to all the problems we have in this troubled world, and He has called us, as Christians, to stand before Him on behalf of others. In prayer, especially doing so by faith, we express our limitations, problems and our desire for God's intervention. In acknowledging our helplessness, God intervenes. Our duty as Christians is to pray by faith, and without ceasing (1 Thessalonians 5:17).

Sharing the Gospel is our Christian Duty

In the words of the Lord, a true born-again, Christ-loving, and God-fearing person will seek to share the Word of God with others (2 Timothy 4:2; 1 Corinthians 9:16). The Lord says that all born-again Christian must be witnesses to the gospel and their lives testify of the working of God's power (Acts 1:8; Mark 16:15-18). The Bible further reminds us that we all received the gift of the Holy Spirit when we first came to Him, even though many people doubt this. The evidence is when the Holy Spirit convicts us, leading to repentance and doing works of obedience (John 6:44; 16:8; Colossians 1:10).

We have heard how some churches teach that the evidence of speaking in tongues is the only sign of one having been filled with the Holy Spirit. Such a teaching is contrary to what the Bible actually says (1 Corinthians 12:30). What we read in the Bible is that speaking in tongues is a visible manifestation of the work of the Holy Spirit in the life of a believer (Acts 2:4, 10:44-46, 19:6; 1 Corinthians 14:22). However, the Bible does not say that speaking in tongues is the only proof that a person has the Holy Spirit. As a matter of fact, there are many examples of people believing in Jesus without mention of them speaking in tongues (Acts 2:41, 8:5-25, 16:31-34, 21:20). As we read in the Bible, the Holy Spirit was given for empowering witnessing activities (Acts 1:8), for fruit bearing (Galatians 5:22-23), and for enabling and supporting the work of ministry (Ephesians 4:11-12).

Through careful study of the Bible, and given my own experiences, any gift from the Spirit requires us to have faith to receive, whether its tongues or the gift of prophecy. As it is, we receive gifts from the Lord as *He wills* (1 Corinthians 12:4-11), not as *we will*. There are some Christians who cannot speak in tongues (1 Corinthians 12:30) but they have received the Holy Spirit. We even had some people who were part of this ministry who couldn't speak in tongues, and yet the Lord sent them out to share Gospel with us. They were part of our witnessing team, meaning they have received power to preach the word (Acts 1:8).

As a final encouragement on this subject, if we don't witness to others, how do we explain to them the hope we have (1 Peter 3:15)? Do we hide the lamp under the bed and not light it up for those in darkness (Matthew 5:15)? If you, as a Christian, do not witness to others, you are either afraid or ashamed of Christ. From my experience, I know such people are full of excuses and they normally struggle with their own faith. In witnessing, you are required to exercise your faith and obedience to Christ. Therefore, sharing the Gospel is faith in action! (2 Timothy 1:7). My brother and sister, in Christ Jesus, I encourage you: come out and be seen and heard and don't let fear of man hinder you from your heavenly reward (Matthew 10:32-33; Acts 5:29).

Rapture Warning: Jesus' Glorious Coming

In a very short, yet powerful vision, on Saturday, August 16, 2014, around 1:00 AM, the Lord showed Charis His glorious coming. In this vision, she was shown the joy and glory that day would hold for those who are prepared. She was simultaneously shown the terror, fear, shame, and hurt that will fall upon many, many unprepared Christians and those in the world. The specific details of this vision and the exact events shown to her were removed from her mind and spirit. She was only allowed to experience an intense fear of God's power and His majesty. She was awakened by her own terrified screaming when she yelled, "Lord please don't make the Rapture happen now; I am scared!" Jaydeen confirmed hearing Charis scream. As soon after this vision ended, Charis woke up crying uncontrollably while closing her face with both hands.

Brethren, we do not commit to a date of Jesus' return, but be warned and fulfill your duties to God (Matthew 24:36; 2 Timothy 4:5).

CHAPTER 7

Prayer is the Key to Solving All Problems – Part I

In this message on prayer, we will share our experiences in order to encourage you to grow stronger in your faith and in your personal relationship with the Lord. This chapter and the next one are by no means exhaustive teachings on this important subject! We are not introducing new doctrines, but fully acknowledging various examples of prayers found in the Bible. As a ministry that has been established by the Lord Himself, we had the privilege and honor of asking the Lord on how to pray effectively for results (James 5:16). We will discuss the Lord's response on this subject in the rest of this chapter. In our opinion, being taught by the Lord is by far the best way to learn about this important subject and others (Luke 24:25-27). We, therefore, give all the glory and honor to God the Father, our Lord Jesus Christ and the Holy Spirit for all the patience, love, help and guidance He provided to us. The Bible teaches us that if we, Christians, don't work for the Kingdom of God and help in gathering (and prayer is key to accomplishing this), then we are essentially working against the Lord and will not enter Heaven (Matthew 12:30; 25:26-30).

Harboring Grudges Hinders Prayer

Many Christians pray and wonder why they receive no answers. From the onset, kindly allow me to introduce some hindrances to prayer; this is very important for us to learn as it is serious in the eyes of the Lord! Often we find brothers and sisters going to the same Church and not talking to each other; they claim to love God, yet they hate their own brethren (1 John 4:20). About two years ago, the Lord sharply rebuked a young man in our ministry for an act of disobedience. After this rebuke, my wife and I counseled the man in an effort to help him change his attitude and understand how his actions had grieved the Lord. Sadly, this young man did not take the Lord's rebuke well, neither did he appreciate our effort in corrective counseling. In a vision to Charis, the Lord showed the condition of his heart; it was revealed that he held a grudge against me and my wife. As a result of his hateful and unforgiving heart, the Lord said that his prayers were rejected and did not reach Heaven (Matthew 5:23-24).

Praying with an unforgiving heart or hatred brings self-condemnation and invites God's judgment (Matthew 6:15). When we pray, we bring our problems, complaints, and troubles before the Lord, seeking His help and wisdom in resolving them (Psalm 50:15; 142:2). However, when we come to the Lord, we should be willing to forgive and let go of any hateful feelings we have towards others even if they sinned against us. We are meant to intercede for them and plead their case for their well-being (Numbers 12:13). In a vision to Charis in 2011, the Lord showed her a lady who harbored hateful feelings against a member of our ministry and was praying for the person to be harmed or destroyed. The lady thought that the Lord would favor her request, but He exposed her guilt and she was ashamed for making such a request. Prayer is meant to plead for mercy and forgiveness, not to try to seek revenge or get even with our enemies (Hebrews 4:16; Matthew 6:12-14).

Why Should We Pray?

In the early stages of our ministry's development, our weekly intercessory prayer sessions were compulsory for all our members; this was according to the Lord's command to us. However, every week we would have members absconding prayers and giving various excuses for their absence. Failing to meet for prayers is not something we should encourage as this affects the rest of the group and leads to more people deserting. Therefore, members of any ministry should guard against this spirit, which is fueled by laziness. After noticing this trend of absenteeism, my wife and I decided to inquire of the Lord after one of the prayer sessions. Generally, situations like these allow for more questions, so we asked the Lord why people were staying away from prayers, and if there is anything that we were doing or saying that was contributing to their absence. The Lord answered that we were not praying enough for the spiritual wellbeing of the individual members and that Satan was attacking them in order to weaken their faith. They needed our prayer support to remain faithful and committed to the will of the Lord. Prior to this correction from the Lord, we prayed as we pleased especially when we needed something. We were not praying consistently or daily for our prayer group. The Bible says that God is a God of order, not confusion (1 Corinthians 14:33). I can tell you, brethren, that the Lord is not pleased with a disorganized Christian. You may call it legalism, but praying just whenever you please (for a need or for someone) is not pleasing to the Lord. The Lord wants to see consistency, urgency, and commitment; we must be organized! In your work situation, do you arrive at work late or leave your workstation in a mess? Probably not! So then, do you expect God to answer your prayers when you pray in a hurry, or when you just pray once in a while for something you need? Prayer must have a purpose, and if so, it should be for something for which we need a solution. We should also bear in mind that prayer is not just about asking, but also includes confession, repentance, praise, and thanksgiving. As it is, we must, therefore, be organized and formal in our approach. Let us have a look at some examples in the Bible.

As children of God, we must realize that God has called us to pray and intercede for our neighbors and our land (Ezekiel 22:30; 1 Timothy 2:1). Abraham was concerned about his nephew Lot's wellbeing, so he prayed and interceded for him and the city where he lived (Sodom) (Genesis 18:22-19:29). Our Lord Jesus Christ prayed for His disciples (John 17:6-26). Moses prayed and interceded for the Israelites (Exodus 32:30-33). Daniel prayed for his people (see Daniel 9) and our Lord's disciples prayed for their ministry work and for one another (Acts 4:24-30). From these examples, we can see that all these prayers were made under various circumstances: for deliverance, for forgiveness, help, healing, and for the salvation of souls. In prayer, the Lord has allowed us to pray for any conceivable human need because only He grants requests and can change what is surely beyond our human abilities (Matthew 19:26; Luke 1:37). Human beings are created to be dependent on God alone (Proverbs 3:5-6; Jeremiah 17:7), for life and everything He supplies to sustain us (2 Corinthians 9:10; Isaiah 55:10), including His Peace (John 14:27).

It is a good habit to set aside proper times for prayer daily. If we have a lazy attitude, we will pray for about 5 minutes before leaving home for work or for some other activity. In my experience, I can tell you, pre-planned or purpose-driven prayers achieve much. A few years ago, before I obeyed God's call for full-time work in the ministry, I used to set aside an hour every morning for prayer, every day before leaving home for work or running an errand. This would give me enough time to talk to God and adequately present my case before Him. As a custom and Biblically-acceptable teaching, I would start by acknowledging God's grace, goodness, and mercy while also acknowledging my own shortcomings and sins (Psalm 19:12).

How Many Times Should We Pray?

The Bible encourages us to pray continually and consistently (1 Thessalonians 5:17). King David wrote: *"Evening, morning and noon I cry out in distress, and He hears my voice"* (Psalm 55:17). Daniel, who was "greatly beloved" by the Lord (Daniel 10:19), was very organized and dedicated; he had his three daily prayer times set and did not allow anything or anyone to interfere with them (Daniel 6:10). In the light of these Scriptures, we asked the Lord directly how many times we ought to pray daily, and how often we should pray for a specific request. In response to our questions, the Lord encouraged us to follow this Scriptural model by praying three times a day. In addition to this, and to confirm His command to us, many other people who requested us to inquire for them from the Lord, were subsequently told by the Lord Himself to pray three times daily. As a Christians, you should, therefore, pray as many times as you deem necessary, but we encourage you to set time aside and pray at least three times a day.

As an encouragement, you may gradually increase your prayers to four or more times a day as you grow in faith and commitment. It is true that you might experience some challenges praying as often as you should be, especially when you are at work. With today's labor laws, most of you are allowed various breaks. You could use these break times to spend some time with God. A few years ago, when I was still in formal employment, I would find a quiet place to pray during my lunch breaks. My habit was that after having lunch, I would slip away from everybody and go to the quiet place to pray.

As a testimony, and in rewarding my efforts, I often experienced joyful moments of God's Presence. On some occasions, I would hear the Lord calling my name, but when I looked I wouldn't see anyone. At times while praying, I would feel somebody touching me, and this brought a strong sense of joy mixed with fear due to the sudden "interruptions". If you commit yourself to spending more time in prayer, you are more likely to hear His Voice guiding you, in addition to receiving some spiritual gifts and fruit, thus enabling you to serve Him even better (Exodus 34:35; John 14:21).

Is Praying in Your Mind Biblical?

When praying, we must release or utter the words. Imagine Jesus praying, saying: *"Lazarus come forth!"* (John 11:43-44) in His mind. Would the people present, especially His disciples, have known what He was praying for? Of course not! There are many prayers recorded in the Bible, and we do not see people only praying in their minds or hearts. We believe in our hearts, but confess prayer with our mouths (Romans 10:9-10). Satan does not know what we are thinking in our minds or hearts, but he receives the full, supernatural force of our faith in Jesus Christ through prayer. As an example, a member of our family was used to praying in her mind. After correcting her several times, she still refused to change this habit. In recognizing her problem, the Lord commanded her to stop praying in her mind, saying that this was an unfruitful exercise. Therefore, to encourage you, if you are unable to pray aloud, praying like Samuel's mother, Hannah, is acceptable and some Christians often do this. The Bible says she was praying in her heart using her mouth to release the words (1 Samuel 1:13). Furthermore, while the Bible encourages us to pray in the spirit or in tongues, we also ought to pray with understanding (1 Corinthians 14:14-15).

When the Lord has given us a promise, should we still continue to pray to receive it? The answer is a resounding "Yes!" We cannot just sit around and wait on God without laboring in prayer. How are we going to appreciate what God has given us if our faith is not going to be tested? Yes, I mean "tested!" Consider how God promised the children of Israel that they would receive the Promised Land (Genesis 13:15, 17). Following this promise, we read in the succeeding Scriptures that they did not receive it on a silver platter like we often expect. Instead, they had to labor in their faith for God's promise by going and taking possession of the land from the inhabitants. God fulfilled His promise to Israel, and this happened through their blood, toil and sweat (Joshua 12:1; 21:43). Likewise, even though Joseph was a young boy when the Lord gave him dreams, and King David was anointed to be king at a young age, their faith was greatly tested before the promises were fulfilled.

In January 2010, when I was unemployed and the Lord promised to bless me with a job, He also promised me a promotion and permanent (full-time) position. However, when I asked Him why I still had not received this promise after working for more than one year, He told me that I did not have enough faith and that I had not been praying hard enough or consistently. In truth, I did not receive all that God promised, but only partially. From my experience, I have learned that God always gives a promise with a test. If we prove to be faithful, He will then bring about the promise (Matthew 25:23; James 1:2-4; Hebrews 11:17). If we lose our patience and become disobedient, we will not receive the full promise (1 Kings 11:38). In the preceding verse, we read that King Jeroboam failed to receive God's promise of a lasting dynasty of kingship. As a result of his disobedience, this king's reward was punishment and the kingdom was taken away from him (1 Kings 13:33-34). In reality, only God knows when we have prayed enough to receive an answer to a request; we must, therefore, be persistent (Luke 11:5-13, 18:1-8).

As an encouragement to you my brethren, if you have not yet received an answer to a prayer request, don't quit, but continue in prayer! I have heard many pastors teaching that after we have prayed for something, we must not pray that request again because that would mean we doubt God. They teach that we must just thank God for it and confess positively that we have already received the request. Most of these "name it and claim it" Christians don't pray faithfully; they just confess, and sadly many of them don't receive the things they asked for. When I was at Bible school in 2009, I even heard some of them demanding of God: "I want what brother or sister so and so has!" This is wrong! We cannot order God around and make Him perform some miracle whenever we need or want something. We should labor for the things we need; such is the nature of things in this life, and in this regard we achieve and receive through prayer (Genesis 3:17; Matthew 21:22). Therefore, this notion of claiming and receiving is false and unscriptural. Didn't our Lord Jesus show us in the Garden of Gethsemane that even though the Father heard Him, He repeated that same prayer three times? (Matthew 26:39-44). In his desperation to receive deliverance from a messenger of Satan, the apostle Paul prayed to the Lord three times until He got an answer (2 Corinthians 12:8-9). He did not unrealistically confess until he received his deliverance from Satan's messenger. What he did, however, is that while his problem persisted, he acknowledged it and continued praying, trusting the Lord to provide an answer.

In my experience, when I genuinely need something from the Lord which is an absolute need, I will not stop praying for it until the request is granted. Now, this does not mean that I cease to pray for the other requests that I have, but the current need would take foremost priority. I can tell you this: the Lord is very pleased when we trust Him to help us! In an uplifting message to my wife after she cried out to the Lord for help over a certain matter, He told her that He loved her expression of faith in Him, and for having faith, He was going to bless her and grant her request. This was a result of persistent prayer and faith.

In the experience relating to our house, which we almost lost to foreclosure, I constantly experienced a heavy burden or restlessness and a strong urge to pray. We should realize that prayer without faith is completely useless, and I can tell you a trying situation can be faith-consuming, allowing for attacks like doubts and feelings of disappointment. When those spiritual symptoms manifested in our situation, the Lord commanded that we (my wife and I, along with our daughter Charis who was about 9 years old at the time) go on a one-day fast. Fasting is not just an expression of humility; it is a faith booster! The day after our fast, the Lord complimented us saying that our faith was strong. We knew from this response that our request was granted, Glory be to God! (Matthew 21:22) He then commanded us to continue praying for the house for a full month. Being faithful and true to His Word, after praying for the full month we asked the Lord if we should still continue to pray for the house. His response through Charis was: *"You, your mother and father do not have to pray for the house; it is in My hands. Your father and mother don't have to do anything else."* Hallelujah! What a great miracle and breakthrough to prayer!

About a week after this relief and confirmation from the Lord, we were served with a notice to appear in court on a given date. This notice caused us great panic, doubt, and confusion. As always, the enemy made a meal of our feelings, causing us to doubt the Lord's earlier promise. In our desperation, we asked the Lord to give us another assurance that He would help us through this trying situation. In a rebuke through Charis, He said: *"Your mother and your father are disobedient! I told your mother and father that they must just pray, for prayer is the key to all problems."* We needed this rebuke to settle our doubts, so we took the Lord's word by faith and prayed as He commanded us. Consequently, our prayers 'swallowed' up the problem, and a few weeks later I received a call from the bank instructing me how to go about settling our debts. The court action was canceled without any word on how this was made possible.

Prayer of Agreement

The Bible reminds us: *"Again, truly I tell you that if two of you on earth agree about anything they ask for, it will be done for them by my Father in heaven."* (Matthew 18:19). Regarding the same house situation we mentioned previously, my family needed a breakthrough so we prayed together in full agreement (Acts 4:24). This happened after we had discussed the problem in order to identify with the situation, and by faith, we stood in agreement. The Lord taught us how to pray in agreement. On some occasions, He would remind us to discuss amongst ourselves the matter that we needed to pray in agreement for. If we agreed in a combined effort of faith (this works like we explained above), He granted us our requests. Similarly, as a ministry, we had a serious need for our own means of transportation due to our service and prayer times ending late, and some of our members living far away from us. We also had the added burden of picking up our children late at night from some relatives who took care of them during the service. After our meetings, sometimes we had to pick up the children under severe inclement weather conditions; this was very difficult for us and our children. However, we were determined to obey the Lord. Having prayed for about three years in corporate agreement as a ministry, the Lord saw our willingness and obedience. He blessed us with two vehicles, and our transportation pains were eased. In Jesus name, I declare truthfully to you, prayer fixes things! We did not need to raise money to buy vehicles through begging for tithes and offerings or conducting fundraising campaigns like we are used to seeing some churches do when they need money. We used 'raw' faith and prayer, and God sent people to provide for our needs. We did not approach these people for help; God sent them to us (Jeremiah 17:5-8). As was the case with Queen Esther and the people of Nineveh, they knew that if everybody was in agreement with them for the common good of the people, God would grant mercy. He did so when they prayed and fasted corporately and faithfully (Esther 4:16; Jonah 3:5).

In one of our meetings, we discussed and agreed as a ministry team to pray for the salvation and deliverance of our immediate family members. It was also our intention to ask the Lord how else we should do it besides just praying. After asking, the Lord commanded that we go on a two-week fast and that we meet together every night for prayer for three hours. This was exactly the model the earlier disciples used (Acts 1:14; 2:46) and their work yielded fruits (Acts 2:47). In obedience, and desperate to see our immediate family members saved, we engaged in deep intercessory prayer. In such prayer, we strongly advise that no young children be present. From our first-hand experience, we have learned that the devil uses children to disrupt prayers through crying and making unnecessary demands for things. This was a lesson we learned deeply after praying one evening with our children present. They were restless, and the Lord rejected that evening's prayers, saying that our prayers did not reach Heaven because of our disobedience. He gave us another chance to offer those prayers on another day. From this discussion, can you see how much God values prayers offered in obedience and with the right attitude? Therefore, do not despise the sacredness of prayer.

Persistent Prayer

In Jesus' narration of the Parable of the Persistent Widow (Luke 18:1-8), I have heard some preachers say that these verses do not refer to persistent prayer. They attempt to interpret the context, and in so doing misunderstand the intention of the analogy; they are clearly wrong. We learned from the Lord that He was referring to persistent prayer. One of my daughters, who is suffering from seasonal allergies, has been praying for deliverance from this annoying condition for about four years now. The Lord acknowledged her prayers, saying that she must continue praying. As I mentioned previously, when I desperately needed a job, I prayed for this request every time during my daily prayer times for a full year. I was desperate and determined and the Lord was not discouraged to hear me praying about the same thing every time. He welcomed me and saw this as effective prayer and He granted my request. He supernaturally answered me and declared the date on which I would receive the job and it happened just like He said. We share our testimony to encourage you, and this is not built on lies but Truth. It is also noteworthy to consider that the Canaanite woman was persistence in her petition to the Lord, and the Lord granted her request (Matthew 15:21-28). So, don't give up praying!

What Should We Pray For?

Many Christians are often faced with the challenge of not knowing what to pray for. As I mentioned before, our prayers must be planned and purpose-driven. We cannot pray for something we don't need; as a matter of fact, our needs and situations motivate us (Daniel 9:2-3). I have heard some people mistakenly saying that prayer is simply a religious practice. While we acknowledge that prayer is related to religion in the Christian context, more accurately it is regarded as fellowshipping with God (1 John 1:3). To clarify this position, the Bible says we as believers are priests (1 Peter 2:9). In the Old Testament, the function of the priest was to present the spiritual and physical needs of the people before God (Deuteronomy 21:5). Therefore, the Lord expects every born-again believer to pray for both believers and non-believers (1 Timothy 2:1), just as Paul and Epaphras did, praying for the spiritual well-being of Christians. Epaphras, a believer in Christ, prayed and interceded for the Colossian brethren (Colossians 4:12). The apostle Paul interceded for the Galatian church saying: *"My little children, for whom I labor in birth again until Christ is formed in you"* (Galatians 4:19 NKJV).

Helping bear the burden of people's salvation, deliverance, and needs is very important. In a request to the Lord, we asked Him to help us with some requests to pray for, and He gave us names of people to pray for. It's been more than four years now, and we are still praying for the same people daily. As it is, out of the fifteen names the Lord gave us, four became born-again Christians and still serve the Lord, but sadly one turned back to the world and later passed away. As believers in the Lord Jesus Christ, we should never stop praying for our parents, brothers, sisters, friends, families, fellow believers, neighbors, colleagues, country, government, church leaders, Christian missions, our communities, criminals and various elements destroying society. Just like the Lord encouraged the Ukrainian believers (in a vision to Charis), He will deliver their land and people if we pray persistently. Remember, prayer gives our land and countrymen an abundant supply of grace and mercy in the presence of the evil (1 John 5:19; 2 Thessalonians 3:3).

The Need to Form a Corporate Prayer Group

As I briefly alluded in the chapter on how this ministry started, our beginnings were very humble. If we are determined and sincere in our walk with God, He will draw like-minded people to us. Often, people may find it challenging to get to church for corporate prayers due to lack of transportation or other problems. This should not be something that leads us to discouragement; you can still invite some brethren over, discuss the needs to be prayed for and then pray! Corporate prayers should not only be at Church. We are not encouraging rebellion towards church authorities, but this is your Christian duty and you are ultimately answerable to the Lord—not to your leaders. If there are no prayer groups at your church, you stay far away from church, or you are unable to participate due to other problems or family issues, we suggest you pray at home with your family or believing neighbors; this is how the apostle Paul encouraged the Roman believers (Romans 16:3-5). You may consider petitioning the Lord to bless you with willing and faithful fellow believers in order to form a prayer group in your immediate neighborhood. I know this might be quite challenging as we have experienced; many people are content with their local church congregation while having no regard for the dying world around them. Their excuse is about their church and leadership. We cannot emphasize this enough: if you find yourself in a non-praying church, get out of there! It is probable that the devil rules there among the worldly and fun-loving Christians. Your faith is personal, and it is, therefore, your responsibility to avail yourselves to God to be used for the common good of the body and the world around us.

Praying in Tongues

Praying in tongues is a very important aspect of prayer that is encouraged in the Scriptures (Romans 8:26; Jude 1:20). As a gift, this is normally the first sign of being baptized in the Holy Spirit (1 Corinthians 14:22). However, as we have mentioned in the "Duties of a True Born-again Christian" chapter, having this gift is not the only proof that a believer has been filled with the Holy Spirit (1 Corinthians 12:30; Acts 21:20).

There are some churches or denominations that discourage their members from praying in tongues. Brethren, I learned in a rebuke from the Lord that we should never discourage people against the teachings of the Word of God. Those who do so encourage rebellion against the Lord, and they will be punished. The Bible tells us that praying in tongues is for self-edification (1 Corinthians 14:4). While we might not know what we are saying when praying in tongues, the Bible says we utter mysteries to God (1 Corinthians 14:2). If these are mysteries, then it is not intended for us or the devil to know what the Spirit says. Therefore, those who cannot pray in tongues should not mock those who exercise their faith and pray in tongues. My question to those critics is this: who qualified you to judge what you don't know or have experienced? In our curiosity about what we say in tongues, my wife and I once asked the Lord through Charis to reveal to us what we say when we are praying in tongues. His answer was gentle and reassuring; He replied saying *"I will not tell you what your mother and father say when they pray in tongues, but I will tell your mother and father in Heaven"*. Bless the Lord, what a promise!

We can conclude on this subject by reiterating that praying in tongues is encouraged in Scripture and should not be undermined (1 Corinthians 14:15, 39). After this reply from the Lord, we realized that had the Lord told us what we say when we pray in tongues, the devil would have known as well, thereby making the above Scripture false that says we speak to God mysteries. There are many worldly people who unjustly criticize the gift of speaking in tongues because they lack spiritual discernment. I, therefore, encourage you not to allow the offensive opinions of the ungodly to disturb you; keep obeying the Scriptures and building yourself up. All Spiritual gifts are for our good, and that is to enable us to serve God better. The Lord gave an encouraging message to a dear sister who was being attacked and ridiculed, saying that the source of those making fun at her is Satan, and He will not allow them to escape punishment.

How Long Should We Pray?

In the Bible, the Lord warns us against engaging in endless babblings and vain repetitions during prayer, iterating the same request over and over again in a single prayer (Matthew 6:7; 23:14). The Lord is here not encouraging only short prayers, since He Himself prayed at great length (Luke 6:12), and He is our example (John 13:15; 1 Peter 2:21). When praying, therefore, don't be in a hurry but take your time as you set forth your request before the Father; God is patiently waiting on you! By faith, ask the Holy Spirit to usher you into His Presence by praising Him and giving thanks: *"Enter His gates with thanksgiving and His courts with praise; give thanks to Him and praise His Name"* (Psalm 100:4). This is how I pray, and you are welcome to follow this model or create your own as the Holy Spirit leads you. After giving thanks and before laying my requests before the Father, I acknowledge my sins in confession, for no one is without sin (1 John 1:8). I then acknowledge God's grace through praise and worship, after which I make my requests known (praying for myself, family, ministry, interceding for others, etc.) (Daniel 9:20).

Remember that no prayer is either too simple or most important, for the Lord judges our hearts and our faith (Luke 18:9-14). Having said this, if you are following a certain prayer model or a formula, do you think God will answer your prayers? God will be looking at the condition of your heart, and whether you have faith in what you are asking for. In my experience, using a model of prayer that worked for someone doesn't guarantee that it will work for you too. Why? Because God appreciates the intentions of a genuine heart and desires that we have a personal; relationship with Him; He does not delight in us being told what to ask and how to ask it. It is similar to a bully sending one of my daughters to me to ask for money that she doesn't really need. In my assessment, and sadly, this kind of formulated prayer does not spring from faith. We need to ask the Lord for true conviction in order to experience change and His generous giving hand.

When Charis was about nine years old, I wrote down three simple prayers for her. I did this only to guide her, and this was accepted by the Lord. I can also recall when Jaydeen, our adopted daughter, was about eight years old; the Lord commanded her mother to write some prayers down for her (for morning, afternoon and evening) since she did not know how to pray and what to say to God in prayer. The Lord accepted these prayers because our motive was to teach, not to dictate. How do I know that the Lord accepted their prayers? He acknowledged in a message to us that they (Charis and Jaydeen) were praying faithfully.

As a final word of encouragement, please don't undermine the value of your own prayers. The Lord is pleased when others pray for us, but if we do not pray for ourselves and just rely on others to pray for us, then we are being lazy and faithless. Some believers even express faith in the prayers of others to God on their behalf, rather than their own prayers! We have known a sister in the Lord who was in the habit of sending out various prayer requests for herself to many other Christians. Simply put, she was "outsourcing" her prayers, and relying on the prayers of others for her. The Lord rebuked her for lacking faith, and He commanded her to pray for herself. The Bible warns us: *"Do not put your trust in princes, in mortal men, who cannot save. When their spirit departs, they return to the ground; on that very day their plans come to nothing"*(Psalm 146:3-4). We are also admonished to *"Trust in Him at all times, you people; pour out your hearts to Him, for God is our refuge"* (Psalm 62:8). Kindled faith is fearless, and a prayer warrior knows how to skillfully handle the powerful weapon of prayer. Don't give up! Be persistent in prayer—the key to solving all problems.

CHAPTER 8

Prayer is the Key to Solving All Problems – Part II

"Pray continually" (1 Thessalonians 5:17).

In a vision the Lord gave to Charis on Friday, June 19, 2015, the Lord led me to reiterate the importance of persistent prayer. In part one of this message, we highlighted the importance of prayer in order to receive results. In this second part, however, we will look at prayer as a spiritual ministry—a service to God and man (Acts 6:4). We serve God in prayer when we acknowledge His grace and power to deliver, protect and provide for us. We serve man in prayer when we acknowledge our sins and the consequences of sin-problems, and seek to love and forgive one another. Prayer is a ministry to God on behalf of the Body of Christ, the world and for our own well-being (1 Timothy 2:1-4).

Vision of Persistent Problems

In this vision, the Lord showed Charis that she and our other children were trapped inside our house by the enemy. In the vision, she was led to understand that my wife and I, along with our three-year-old daughter managed to escape but left the older children to find their way out by themselves. When the older children realized that they were all alone, they too tried to escape using all the available exits. Because of the persistent charging of the enemy, who had secured all the escape routes with determined demonic guards and snakes, the children were left totally paralyzed with fear and at the mercy of the enemy. When Charis finally managed to briefly get away from the enemy, she was shown that some of the children were captured and hanged. She had desperately tried to encourage them not to give up their faith in the Lord, but to fight in order to secure their salvation. Soon after the vision ended, the Lord spoke and said, *"Pray, pray, pray always. Pray no matter what!"*

In interpreting this message, the Lord says that everyone will have to escape the attacks and snares of Satan using his own faith (Ezekiel 18:20; Jeremiah 31:30). He also said that instead of panicking and trying to run from our problems, we should turn to Him in prayer and ask for help. If we run, the problems will only multiply, resulting in not being able to escape from Satan's traps and failing totally in our faith, ultimately suffering eternal consequences.

Prayer Activates Faith

As is commonly known, prayer releases our faith in God's ability to show us mercy and to help us in our troubles and times of need (Luke 18:1-8). In prayer, we put our trust (faith) and lay our burden on God. In His assurance to us, the Lord gives us His peace to comfort us while we are waiting for His timely solution (Matthew 11:29-30; John 14:27). In other words, His peace is an expression of His care for us (1 Peter 5:7). Brethren, we must realize that when we doubt God, panic will overwhelm us and suffocate our faith. As a result, we will not embrace or enjoy His peace, neither can we expect an answer from Him (James 1:6-7; Mark 11:24).

There are many reasons why the Lord does not answer prayers. Some of the stumbling blocks include: doubt (James 1:6-7), sinful living and unfaithfulness in our service to God (John 9:31; 1 Peter 3:7), grudges or unforgiveness (Matthew 5:23-24), and not being persistent in prayer (Luke 18:1-8; Romans 12:12; Colossians 4:2-6). From the Scriptures, we see the following specific examples:

- When some of the Israelites doubted God's promises, He denied them entry into the Promised Land (Numbers 14:20-30).
- God rejected Saul's prayers due to His disobedience (1 Samuel 28:6).
- King David was not driven by malice, grudges or unforgiveness towards Saul who persecuted Him, but his willingness to forgive King Saul and leave him in the hands of the Lord brought honor to God who is the Supreme Judge (1 Samuel 26:9-11). This noble act secured the Lord's promise of giving the throne of Israel to David (1 Samuel 15:28).
- King Hezekiah's persistence in prayer resulted in God answering his prayer by delivering him and his army from the arrogant Assyrian forces (Isaiah 38:5-6).

In a remarkable way, God releases His promises first to support our faith to trust in Him, and as we obey while trusting in Him, He fulfills the promises (Genesis 12:2). As it is, these promises are only fulfilled after an experience of faith, hardship and test (Genesis 22:1; Hebrews 6:15). From the above Scriptures, it becomes apparent that God uses our faith, patience and our obedience in fulfilling His promises.

God's Timing in Answering Prayer

In a desperate tone, someone once wrote me an email saying that he did not receive any answers to his prayers because God does not care about him. In response, the Lord revealed that this person lived in disobedience and that he was being worldly and impatient. On the subject of lacking patience, I also had to endure a rebuke from the

Lord about five years ago for being impatient and lacking faith. My habit was constantly asking the Lord through Charis when I would receive a promise. Instead, He encouraged me to continue praying and reassured me that He had not forgotten about His promises and my requests (2 Peter 3:9). Persistent prayer is, therefore, an expression of faith, humility and patience, and at the appointed time God will answer, just like He remembered Joseph (Genesis 41:14).

With so much deception swirling around and people being so desperate for fame and fortune, we must be very careful as there are some preachers who go about demanding money from people, claiming that they have some special anointing to help solve our problems as if they have a special relationship with God. You should depend on your own faith and prayers; we already have learned how the prayer of agreement works. Don't act desperately and run to people to seek God on your behalf when you have problems. Instead, you should trust the Lord and use that situation to express your faith in the Him. Humble yourself and wait on the Lord, He will hear your heart and provide. God is no respecter of any person (Acts 10:34; Romans 2:11). In this walk of faith, we are all called to endure individually and be tested and readied by God for ministry service and Kingdom approval (1 Peter 1:6-8).

While it is true that no one can say exactly when God will answer a prayer request, it is also true that He will answer us if we prove faithful to him in persistent prayer. We should always expect Him to answer us no matter how long we wait (Matthew 21:22). If we pray aimlessly, that is without adding faith to our prayer and a sense of desperation for the answer to our request, we may not have our prayer answered. I once trusted the Lord to bless me with a job promotion because this would have saved me from transport problems and having to work awkward shifts. However, I did not receive the answer that I expected due to not being persistent in prayer, and my heart was also on another job. I was divided having a double interest: the prospect of a new job and the promise of a promotion. In my indecisiveness, I was interested in either opportunity, and this led to me losing out on both. Brethren, when we are divided in what we want, God will not choose for us; we must make a firm decision and be undivided in our request. We cannot simply act like children who want this and later decide that we need something else. No! With the Lord, we must be resolute in our choice as this shows faith and destiny (2 Kings 20:1-6).

As an emphasis, an answer to our prayers is dependent on how desperately we want that something and this will determine how patient we will be until God comes through for us. As to how long the Lord will take to grant our request, He does so when it is needed and when we have pleased Him in our diligence and obedience (Daniel 10:11-13). The preceding Scripture declares that Daniel's prayer was immediately heard and answered, unbeknown to him. As an expression of his desperation, Daniel fasted for 21 days to show his faith and his need for God's answer. Satan, who always manages to delay and detain our answers from God, was overcome by Daniel's faith and persistence (Daniel 10:2), and after 21 days his answer was released. How many of us set a date for God to answer our prayers, and if He does not answer us by that date we give up?

The greater the problem we face, the more faith and determination or interest we must show to have our request granted (Matthew 15:21-28; Luke 8:43-48). Let us therefore not give up praying, for only therein can we access God's mercy, deliverance, and provisions. With a humble heart and a sincere faith, God will not neglect to answer our prayers (Isaiah 65:24), but if we give ourselves to complaining, He will not bring to birth the plans He has for each one of us (Numbers 14:20-23; Jeremiah 29:11). His precious promises serve as an incentive for us to grow in our faith, and after we are proved faithful and obedient, God in His wisdom releases these promises for us. However, the faithless He excludes from His promises (Hebrews 4:3). Rest in the Lord's faithfulness and always pray, no matter what! However compelling the circumstances, still pray. Prayer is the key in the hand of faith to unlock God's blessings and give you victory.

CHAPTER 9

The Eternal Benefit of Godly Correction

"So you, son of man: I have made you a watchman for the house of Israel; therefore you shall hear a word from My mouth and warn them for Me. When I say to the wicked, 'O wicked man, you shall surely die!' and you do not speak to warn the wicked from his way, that wicked man shall die in his iniquity; but his blood I will require at your hand. Nevertheless, if you warn the wicked to turn from his way, and he does not turn from his way, he shall die in his iniquity; but you have delivered your soul" (Ezekiel 33:7-9 NKJV).

Human lives are fundamentally shaped by trials, errors, and corrections. For these reasons, the Lord God has commanded believers to rebuke sin and expose error through the Scriptures, in order to prepare us for perfection and conformity to His righteous ways (Ephesians 5:11; 2 Timothy 2:24-26; 4:2; Titus 1:9-14). Before we proceed with this message, we wanted to share with you a warning the Lord gave us on the dangers of swearing.

Warning from the Lord against the Spirit of Swearing

Vision Given to Claudia on April 1, 2015

The Lord Jesus Christ appeared in a vision to my eight-year-old daughter, Claudia, on April 1, 2015, and warned her on the dangers of swearing. Dressed in a pure white robe and covered in light, the Lord warned Claudia not to swear. In this vision, she pleaded for forgiveness from the Lord for swearing. He went on to tell her that if she and Jaydeen (our other daughter) continue in this sin of swearing, they would go to hell forever and that they would never get to see Charis (our eldest daughter) and the rest of the family. While this was a direct warning to Claudia, the Lord commanded us to share this message with everyone and take heed of this warning.

In today's society, swearing, cursing, cussing, and using profane and filthy language have become acceptable practices, and many people find it natural to use offensive words as a way to express themselves. The Bible clearly says that we must consider how to encourage and build up one another in the Lord; we are clearly warned not to allow corrupt talk to come out of our mouths (Ephesians 4:29). Before I came to the Lord, I was likewise corrupted by swearing. I am not ashamed to share with you that I was seriously warned by the Lord not to swear to people or animals. We should keep our tongues free from profanity, insulting, or using abusive language to others (Ephesians 5:4-6). As a watchman to your spiritual wellbeing, please be warned and repent from this wickedness that has become prevalent in our society. We are expected to treat others with respect and dignity, not allowing ourselves to be deceived by pride or corrupted by worldly influences and positions of power. Remember that you reap what you sow (Job 4:8; Galatians 6:7), and that *"for every idle word men may speak, they will give account of it in the Day of Judgment. For by your words you will be justified, and by your words you will be condemned"* (Matthew 12:36-37 NKJV). Since we are all created in God's image (Genesis 1:27), we should not harbor hate or resentment, but love people and pray for those who curse us and mistreat us! (Matthew 5:44; Luke 6:28).

Rebuking Christians for Error

In my experience as a minister of the Gospel, I have had the opportunity to be sent by the Lord to Christian brethren, including pastors, who are walking in disobedience. Sadly, many of them did not respond humbly to the Lord's rebuke, yet these are the same believers who expect their flock and unbelievers to submit to rebukes and corrections from them. The Bible tells us: *"The ear that hears the rebukes of life will abide among the wise. He who disdains instruction despises his own soul, but he who heeds rebuke gets understanding"* (Proverbs 15:31-32 NKJV). God uses those on the inside, and not outsiders, to express His way (Galatians 2:11; 1 Peter 4:17; Titus 1:9-14). This explanation comes in response to letters from members of the body who questioned our work. As we explain below, the work of this ministry and others is a God-ordained function within the body. Our motive is not to police others or to be elevated as being "super special"—we fear God (Philippians 2:3). Our motivation is to encourage those who spread error to repent and the lost sheep to return so that both may be saved (Ezekiel 3:18-21). Christians who continue to live in their sin gain a fruitless life in Christ and He has no use for them in His service (Matthew 3:10; 5:13). The Lord Jesus Christ says that such people are selective in their obedience to Him, and this will only earn them His wrath (Romans 1:18; 2:5-11). Therefore, do not hate those who speak corrective truth to you in the name of the Lord (Amos 5:10).

Confronting and Challenging Error in the Body

As a responsible Ministry under submission to Jesus Christ, we would like to briefly explain why we are warning members of the Body of Christ against teachings that are destroying our relationship with the Lord. Earlier in 2015, we wrote, by instruction from the

Lord, about "Prosperity Prophets", and in prior messages, the Lord had instructed us to write about "Prosperity Teachers", "Pastors Repent", "False Witness" and many other subjects which are available for reading on our website. Through these messages, the Lord also gave important warnings. Whether you believe us or not remains a matter of your faith and conviction, but we were directly commanded by the Lord Jesus Christ to write and warn the church against the teachings of certain prominent individuals in the Church.

As it is, many non-discerning Christians dislike us for warning the Church against false teachings. Even though the Lord God of Truth has mandated us to expose false teachers and their teachings, some people accuse us of "judging". Brethren, please discern for yourselves from what we have written—are we judging people or their message? The truth of the matter is that we are not driven by any malice or jealousy, and we don't judge people (Matthew 25:31-46; John 5:22). What we do is Biblically judge their message and offer you the opportunity to do likewise (1 Corinthians 14:29). We present to you the choice to humble yourself, pray and follow your conscience in discerning Biblical truth.

While these teachers might be doing a wonderful job in some of their ministry commitments, and doing good deeds for God is commendable, it is sinful and dangerous to accept human opinions and erroneous doctrines which deviate from the Scriptures. Therefore, if we allow their work to go unchallenged we would not be operating from the Holy Spirit's conviction. We would be literally dead in our faith if we dare not challenge the Scriptural position of their teachings. The Bible clearly warns us on the dangers of false teachings or "yeast" (Matthew 16:6; Galatians 5:9). We should further realize that it is equally sinful and dangerous to blindly jump to the defense of some Bible teachers you love, especially when their teachings are contrary to Scripture. It is worth reading how Korah, Dathan, Abiram and all their followers were destroyed by the Lord when they rebelled in error! (Numbers 16:1-40). We are instructed to *"Depart now from the tents of these wicked men! Touch nothing of theirs, lest you be consumed in all their sins"* (Numbers 16:26 NKJV).

When we stand up in defense of someone who spreads error, we are foolishly blinding that person and also encouraging rebellion against God. The Lord warns us not to take human sides but to side with the Truth (John 18:37). Two of our ministry members learned first-hand not to defend men who are spreading error in the body of Christ. The Lord, through a serious rebuke, promised them punishment. However, through prayer, humility, and sincere repentance, they were forgiven and delivered from those demons associated with such false teachings. Are you willing to die eternally for a "man of God" whose wickedness you know nothing about because you "love" them? Or are you willing to surrender to God's great love in correcting you, so that you may be saved (Hebrews 12:6; Proverbs 3:12)?

God judges the facts of our truthful conduct and not how we feel about something or someone. It is true that we sometimes can become emotionally involved with people, but that should not make us overlook truth and entertain error. Today, the practice in the body is unification or ecumenism, with smaller ministries being annexed to promote a single ministry's influence nationally and internationally. Such acquisitions are often achieved by selling the credibility of the founding member and his ministry's achievements. I have seen some pastors giving up their calling and churches so as to become part of a bigger network of churches. This shift is undoubtedly meant to gain more popularity and power, members and of course, money. This move is most likely benefiting the leaders, not the flock. What the flock needs is the Holy Spirit and more of God in their lives in order to bear godly fruits. On some social media platforms, some Christians are so blinded by the 'superstar syndrome' of some pastors, that they rudely slander other believers in order to receive approval and acceptance from these pastors. This kind of behavior does not earn God's approval. God never intended for Christians to play the game of being better than others (Matthew 20:26) just because of having better resources. No! God forbid, no amount of status, riches or influence saves souls. We are saved by Jesus and His humble experience of the cross. I choose that above all.

Loyalty to Christ, Not Man

The practice of apologetics to boldly challenge error and falsehood in the body of Christ, and to rebuke those who spread confusion in the body, has been practiced in the church since the earlier times (2 Timothy 2:16-18; 3 John 1: 9-10). From Scripture, we see Paul rebuking Peter for sowing confusion; he did so to uphold the truth while correcting Peter. He was not simply considering Peter's reputation (Galatians 2:11-14). As believers in Christ, there should be no master-servant relationship among us, but Christ is the Master and we are all humble servants who are enslaved to the truth (1 Corinthians 7:22). Therefore, as mere mortals, we are all imperfect and God is using His word to perfect our ways. We who preach and teach the Word are not above it. We too must submit in humility and obedience to corrections and warnings from the Word of God (James 3:1; 1 Corinthians 9:27).

Therefore, in our humble work, we don't take it upon ourselves to 'police' the church. It is the Lord who calls, commands and reveals the disturbing trends in the body prophetically. As a result of our work and calling, we have become very unpopular, but the Lord in an encouraging message to us said that not everybody in the world will reject our message. We are not seeking a name for ourselves, neither are we canvassing for loyalty. As it is, we have no appetite for power games. In our work, we humbly preach Christ and His truth, allowing His Word to judge and discern our motives in our message to you.

About five years ago soon after we launched this ministry, I worked happily together with some wonderful and God-fearing men and women of God. In their love for us, these precious brethren unselfishly shared many material things with us, helping us with much-needed resources for our ministry work. In the Lord's great love, He issued some strong messages of corrections and rebukes to some of these brethren. Until today, many of them regretted saying that this was my thank you to them; but in actual fact, correction from error is more precious than gold for the reward thereof is eternal life (Psalm 19:9-11). The trend most people follow today is to simply ignore someone's mistakes and supposedly pray for them. What effect would my prayer have if I don't show my love to my brother by correcting them? Let me put it this way, what we may benefit materially from members of the body is not as important as their obedience to the Lord (1 Samuel 15:22) and their salvation.

The truth is priceless, immeasurable and incomparable! What the Lord did, is He gave them messages to save and deliver them from their sin (Lamentations 2:14). Admittedly, at first I ignored some bad yeast in their teachings not wishing to upset them, but when some concerned and discerning brethren emailed me inquiring about some questionable teachings from some of those brethren, I could not ignore and compromise on the value of truth. We carefully compared their teachings in the light of the Scriptures and I wrote to some of them with the aim of calling attention to the questionable teachings.

After being rejected, I set out praying and the Lord reminded me not to be afraid to rebuke people when I see them corrupting His word (Leviticus 19:17). I obeyed the Lord and challenged these brethren privately on some of the things they were teaching, and as would be expected, their pride stood in the way and their natural choice was to avoid contact or association with me. However, in contrast, there have been equally humble brothers and sisters who have continued with us despite sharp rebukes from the Lord, and they have been supporting this ministry and our message in every way. These precious brethren looked beyond their own feelings, but acknowledged their shortcomings and allowed truth from Jesus Christ to convict and correct them. In truth, our humility is tested by our submission to a word of correction (Psalm 139:23-25; 141:5).

Finally dear brethren, do not be like mockers who hate, reject, abuse, and insult those who give them godly correction intended to bless and ward them away from enslavement to the enemy (Proverbs 9:7; Matthew 21:33-46; Luke 20:9-19, Mark 12:1-12). Rather, choose to be wise men and women of God who are receptive to godly correction which is able to lead you away from error and paves the way to eternal life (Proverbs 9:8; 17:10).

Vision of a Man Who Despised Warning

Given to Charis on May 24, 2013

"I was shown a vision of one of my father's deceased friends who died in a tragic car accident in 2012. I was shown a conversation my father had with this man some time ago. After sharing this vision with my father, he confirmed that he had such a conversation with his deceased friend. I saw uncle G (My father's friend) coming into our living room, and he exchanged greetings with my father. Uncle G spoke up telling my father, "I feel that I am going to die because the Lord confirmed it to me in a dream." After saying this, I heard my father say, "G, since the Lord warned you that you are going to die, I beg you to make your life right with the Him so that you may go to Heaven when you die. You are a good-hearted person and the Lord is going to bless you." I then saw uncle G smiling at my father as if saying "not now," and he disappeared".

Clarification on This Vision

I knew this friend for many years, since high school in fact. I shared an apartment with him and his wife for many years. During my worldly ways, we drank, smoked and faced similar struggles together. When I gave my heart to the Lord, my friend G did the same a few weeks after me. A few months after committing to the Lord, and after he got a new job, he returned to his old ways. When he discontinued visiting me regularly, I knew that something was not right and I prayed interceding for him. A few days later, the Lord showed me in a dream that he had started drinking alcohol again. The next available Saturday, I went to his house to surprise him. I also wanted to confirm for myself if he was really drinking again. We had a private conversation, and he admitted that he had started drinking again. He also expressed appreciation for my effort and said that he needed more time to think. Sadly, he waited way too long to make up his mind about following the Lord. He drowned himself in the bottle and was suddenly caught by death's surprise.

Soon after I heard about his tragic death, I always wanted to know if he had an opportunity to make right with the Lord before he died. After a conversation with his wife a few days following his death, she seemed convinced that he might have had an opportunity to make right a few seconds before he died. I doubted her while hoping that maybe there was a chance he made right with God.

However, I take this vision as a confirmation of his eternal fate, and I have abandoned all hope of ever seeing my friend and brother again. A month before he died, he had come to me exactly as in the vision. He told me his plans and I repeatedly told him to commit his plans and ways into the hands of the Lord, but he was absorbed by the things he still wanted to do.

I appeal to you, dear reader: the Lord has purposely given this vision and permitted us to share it with you. If you know someone or you are that someone, who banks on time to make right with God, that time is now (2 Corinthians 6:12). God has set for you one day, and it is today (Matthew 6:34; James 4:13-17; Hebrews 4:7). Get out of your backslidden state and stop drinking and pursuing worldly things. This vision might not be as explosive as you would have wanted it, but it's a warning.

CHAPTER 10

Obedience through Test

Lord, I Need Your Test to Prove My Love to You!

In this chapter, we will share a compelling testimony on testing and how the Lord Jesus Christ drew our attention to the fruit of the Holy Spirit. Having been a Christian for over 20 years, I have seen and met many believers who despise tests, and some of them don't realize that testing is necessary and is meant for our growth and expression of love to the Lord. As the apostle Paul observed, tests produce the fruit of the Spirit in us (Romans 5:3-5). Most of us have read a newspaper article or storybook how a hero showed his love to someone, even to the point of death. This might be a true gesture of love, and we should appreciate that, but the death of Jesus Christ on the cross for our sins is even more priceless as it holds an eternal benefit to the entire human race (John 3:16). This is the love we should embrace willingly and without restraint. In sharing our testimony, we do not intend to bring focus to ourselves, but rather to prove the inerrancy and authoritative nature of God's Word. All evidence of truth must be Scripturally-relevant and grounded on God's Word. I, therefore, encourage you strongly in the lord Jesus Christ to ponder this strong Scriptural evidence and ready yourself to serve the Lord. We are all called to put our faith and love for the Lord to the test, through service and self- sacrifice. May the Spirit of the Living God guide and lead you into all His truth.

Tests Expose Our Hidden Weaknesses and Make Room for New Fruit

Truthfully, the tests that we pass through and those experienced by some individuals in the Bible were not necessarily pleasant experiences (Deuteronomy 8:2). Those being tested cried out to God for help! (Job 19:7; 30:20; Psalm 69:29). In this life, it is difficult to imagine how it would be if there was no test to bring out pain, excitement to show triumph, love to show belonging, and hurt to express a need for forgiveness. In the absence of the above, if there were no uncertainties and disruptions, the human experience would be meaningless, rigid, and without an adventure. When God placed the human race on the earth, He made us remember things we did in the past. However, He hid from us knowing the future outright, so that we might discover the future through Him (Genesis 2:16-17; Isaiah 46:10). To the human race, the future is uncertain, and by experiencing life, we discover our faults, the truth about things, and God's grace in helping us cope with life's uncertainties (Isaiah 58:11; Psalm 32:8). Therefore, the door of tests opens our lives to character building and brings our hidden weaknesses out for us to acknowledge and work on them. As humans, we grow and learn more about ourselves by self-discovery and through environmental pressures. Going through tests exposes our inner attitude and helps measure how much we value God, others and appreciate life.

Because we cannot foresee the future, the path ahead of us is hidden and uncertain, and we consciously sense the pain or excitement of our journey through life. When the going gets tough, we either decide to continue on our own or find help from God or others to ease the burden of our life's journey. If we have built our lives through the experiences, sacrifices, and pain of others before us, this makes the journey through life more comfortable and with less effort. Unfortunately, when we are "cushioned" from the harsh realities of life or are building on someone's foundation, we may become complacent and think that we do no need God because we can do everything by ourselves or through the help of others. Such a faithless attitude promotes spiritual laziness while developing bad fruit and attitudes which demons feast on to keep the person captive. Modern society, especially in the developed countries and urban cities across the world, is trapped in the comfort of effortless enjoyment of life's luxuries because we can buy our way through. Under such conditions of ease, experiencing life through test helps to develop appreciation, gratitude, humility, and empathy as the hardships can help us identify with those needy in society and, hopefully, be moved to offer help where needed.

Today's Christians, especially those who have embraced the feel-good, prosperity gospel, regard God as our servant whom we demand to help us when tests and trials strike us. Similarly, there are some fine and prestigious Bible institutions today, and in my experience, the individuals they have produced have the knowledge and the qualification on paper, but the heart is running without the real fruit of truth and of service to advance the Christian course. Conversely, we have a few Churches where the Bible is fully taught and the knowledge of the Word of God is at a peak with people using Scriptural references to comfort themselves and share with others as they await the soon return of the Lord—this is where we ought to be.

Jesus Christ our Supreme Example and Model for Obedience

Our Lord Jesus Christ was the only Person not born to uncertainty because He knew the arduous road that He would travel through this life; this was set out for Him from the foundation of the world through eternity (Ephesians 1:4, 1 Peter 1:20). His life unfolded as He willed it, and it turned out to be the way He purposely chose (John 10:18; 12:23-28; Luke 22:10-13, 20:19-26). Based on these Scriptural examples, there was nothing the Lord did not know. He purposely chose the Cross, including the suffering and the humiliation associated with it (John 10:17-18). He boldly and fearlessly declared: *"I came to this hour"* (John 12:27). The Lord's fearless attitude showed purpose, destiny and a clear intent on accomplishing what He came here for, which is to redeem man from hell and rise again to go and prepare a place of rest for us, Hallelujah! (John 14:3).

He clothed Himself with the Fruit of the Spirit, most notably He was humble and became a servant to experience human pain, suffering, and shame (Philippians 2:6-11). The life and suffering of Christ were well chronicled in the book of Isaiah (Isaiah 53, for example) and many other passages in the Bible. This was a powerful statement of God saying: "I love My creation!" This complete work of the cross and our Lord's resurrection ushered in a new dispensation in the order of creation. Through it, we see that this current state of all creation, including Heaven, is passing and a renewal is looming (Matthew 24:35; Romans 8: 19-23). All things are to be renewed and reconciled through Christ (Colossians 1:20), Who learned obedience through the things He suffered (Hebrews 5:8).

Obedience to God comes at the price of denying self in order to serve God. When we must obey, there must be no "what about me?" It is all about giving ourselves over for the benefit of others; this is the principle of the Kingdom of God (Philippians 2:3). Because we are in service to God, we can trust Him to provide for all our needs (Philippians 4:19). Hardships, which help reveal the condition of the heart, therefore, produce character (either negatively or positively) in our submission to God. Every born-again believer in Christ has a unique opportunity to experience salvation through test and service to God and others. Our salvation does not just come through repentance; it is also revealed through ministry service, obedience and the bearing of fruit (John 15:1-15). As it is, our repentance must lead us to bear fruit to serve God and others (Matthew 13:8). In a strongly worded message to his hearers John the Baptist said: *"The ax is already at the root of the trees, and every tree that does not produce good fruit will be cut down and thrown into the fire"* (Matthew 3:10). To avoid being "axed", we must resolve to serve Him faithfully through the fruit of the Holy Spirit.

The Fruit of the Holy Spirit: A Must-have for Believers

Jesus Christ our Lord and Savior displayed all the fruit of the Holy spirit through His life. His conception through the Holy Spirit had the 'seed' of the Fruit present to produce fruit (Luke 2:51-52). The fruit of the Spirit attracts both man and God to us, and as such our Lord did this. Our testimony and discipleship are shown not just through our knowledge of God's Word, but through the fruit as well (John 13:35, Acts 4:13). Unsaved people are only attracted by the fruit we bear; they look for the fruit in us first before believing our witness and testimony, and then they decide to obey or despise the Lord. The Holy Fruit of the Holy Spirit encompasses very high virtues of excellence and perfection. Biblically, the God-Head is known through these eminent qualities, and Christ Jesus endows those He has called with these fruits (John 15:5). When we live by the fruit of the Holy Spirit, there is no law to convict or find the Holy Spirit guilty, because no unrighteousness, sin or prejudice is found in love. He, the Holy Spirit, being in us produces selfless justice and He defends the weak through the strong virtue of love (Romans 8:8-10,

Galatians 5:22-25). We must follow the Spirit and His law of love will conquer all human situations.

How the Fruit Grows in a Believer

Every born-again believer who received the baptism of the Holy Spirit by faith should bear fruit in their lives (John 15:8). Our Lord Jesus said that the Holy Spirit would testify about Him and bring glory to Him (John 16:13). We will, therefore, bear much fruit if we are saved and apply the Word of God in our lives (John 15:7). As believers, why do we often desire the gifts more than the fruit of the Holy Spirit? From my experience, it's mostly because we want the power to attract others to us and have convincing signs. While this is good, the Lord has also given the Fruit of the Spirit in the body and to individual believers to minister and display His character to humanity. Life is uncertain and full of pain and suffering, but the Fruit of the Holy Spirit gives us hope and helps us cope with life. As I alluded earlier, followers of Christ are identified by the fruits of holiness. Further below we will attempt to show how God used tests to help us appreciate the work of the Holy Spirit in our lives, resulting in fruit-bearing.

Tests and Trials Produce Fruit of the Holy Spirit

If we commit ourselves to following and obeying the Lord Jesus Christ, we will face and attract persecutions (Matthew 5:11; 2 Timothy 3:12). This is part of the Christian experience because the cross requires us to die to self (Matthew 7:13). This is an essential Christian training, just like the Lord Jesus was tried and tested by Satan himself (Matthew 4). Now, He didn't need to learn obedience; He simply had to show His obedience and submission to God the Father (Hebrews 5:8). The word 'learned' in the above Scripture refers to Him accepting suffering, rather than being tested to learn. If we submit to God, He promises to do the pruning and impartation of fruits while changing our attitudes (John 15:1).

When we go through tests and trials, we may experience pain, whether physical or emotional or both. None of us likes the discomfort of pain, especially emotional pain, which is much more unbearable because it leaves us without the fruit of peace. I have observed that every bad fruit is manifested when a person does not have peace within. The good news is that words of comfort can heal the heart of emotional pain and revive peace (Proverbs 16:24).

God Gives through People

The Bible clearly states that every virtue and gift from the Holy Spirit operates outside the human will; He distributes to each one individually as He wills, not as we want (1 Corinthians 12:11). In other words, we cannot simply force the Holy Spirit to conjure up a gift or fruit. He manifests as we willingly submit to His guidance and He does this to minister to a need in honor to God. Therefore, when the fruit of the Holy Spirit is manifested, it results in the growth of ministry, and the Lord wants to use believers to meet people's needs through the fruit of the Holy Spirit.

Kindly allow me to share the following testimony. Before I got the job the Lord promised and subsequently provided back in February 2010, we were totally broke financially. My wife and I discussed the matter, weighing the options of where and to whom we could go for help. We decided to just use our faith and pray in agreement, asking the Lord to provide me with 'taxi-fare' to attend my scheduled interview. Since the Lord was speaking to us regularly and knew what I needed the money for, we decided to inquire of Him. When He visited Charis that evening, she asked Him: "Lord

Jesus Christ, my father says he must go for an interview tomorrow, and he is asking if the Lord can please provide taxi-fare for him." The Lord replied, saying: *"I will send someone today to bring your father money [indicating the amount] for his interview".* The next day, my wife's friend, who is not a born-again Christian, came over for a visit. Remember, the Lord did not reveal the identity of the person He promised to send to us. My wife's friend reached for her purse and took out the amount money we believed the Lord for, without my wife asking her for it. This moved my wife into a rapturous joy without divulging to her why she was excited. Surely, it was not the money that stirred our excitement, but the faithful fulfillment of the Lord's promise. In this situation, the Lord used the gift of giving through an unsaved person to meet a need. When we later revealed to this precious woman how the Lord used her, she was moved into tears and a feeling of being unworthy to be used so innocently by the Almighty.

We had a separate teaching from the Lord on how He chooses to bless. In my experience, the Lord may choose to bless us directly with the thing we trusted Him for, and in rewarding us He would surprise us and this gift from Him is always unexpected. In 2011, a sister in our ministry decided to bless my wife and me with a sum of money. While we had money of our own, and being conscience of the spirit of greed, we decided to ask the Lord through Charis if we could take the money from the sister. The Lord answered saying, *"Your father may take the money [indicating the amount] from My daughter Grace (not real name). It is not My daughter Grace blessing your father; it is Me".*

Bad Fruit is caused by Satan

In yet another teaching, this time the Lord revealed to us that screaming which arises out of anger comes from the devil. In discouraging this kind of behavior, He rebuked a sister who was in the habit of screaming in anger, saying: *"My daughter Sue (not real name) must not scream; it is from the DEVIL. My daughter Sue must have a spirit of love"*. I have added this to warn those mothers and fathers who like screaming to their children and others. The Bible talks about Satan being the king of terror (Job 18:14), and he uses screaming to induce fear and submission. So, be careful not to be angry and start yelling at the top of your voice! In contrast, the Lord gives peace to drive away fear. As a reminder, remember we cannot just switch the fruit of the Spirit "on" or "off". The Holy Spirit chooses to manifest, influence and work through an obedient, discerning, and a God-fearing child of God. In a message to me, the Lord told me that obedience and faithfulness are very pleasing to Him because these are an expression of our Love for Him.

The Impartation of the Fruit of Faithfulness and Patience through Test

Let us briefly examine the Scriptures to learn how God brought forth the fruit of faithfulness and patience through test in some of His most notable servants. The Bible says that God tested Abraham through his willingness to obey Him and sacrifice Isaac (Hebrews 11:17). For Abraham to pass the test God gave Him, he had to obey submissively and by faith. We have had a firsthand experience that the test given by the Lord is not always easy. It involves a selfless giving and submission to His will. I will briefly share later how we were subjected to test by the Lord. Abraham, the patriarch, was called by God to leave his father's land (Hebrews 11:8) and to prove his obedience to God who subjected him to testing (Genesis 22). In teaching Abraham patience, the Lord gave him promises which we might not be able to wait for so long. After his faith endured, Abraham received God's promise (Hebrews 6:15).

Considering a few more examples of test in the Bible, the children of Israel were tested when God took them through the wilderness (Exodus 15). Even so, our Lord Jesus Christ was tested (Matthew 4). Job was also tested (Job 1), and so was the prophet Daniel and his friends (Daniel 6:16-28; Daniel 3:1-30). In addition, faithful women of God like Esther and Ruth endured test. Therefore, from the above examples, every man or woman of God who walks in obedience to Him will be tested. Testing might even happen at the expense of one's life and against one's personal interest (Luke 17:33 and Luke 14)—even to the point of death (Revelation 2:10). In this kind of experience, we willingly and submissively set our own goals aside to serve the greater good of others (Galatians 5:13).

Nowadays there seems to be some kind of competition among some Christians in their pursuit of worldly wealth. I can recall when I attended Bible school classes at a well-known charismatic church. We were encouraged to trust God for wealth with Scriptures being cited out of context to promote avarice. Just because God chose to bless Abraham and others, we were taught to claim the same right. Brethren, this kind of teaching elevates and inflates needs, more than holy living. In my understanding, this teaching runs similar to the one the prophet Jeremiah confronted when he challenged the "peace preachers" of his day (Jeremiah 28:9). Satan has set a trap and blindfolded many believers into believing that riches is what God wants for them. It is a shameful thing to show off our godliness through our wealth when we have neighbors who are starving. The question we should ask ourselves is, do we accumulate wealth to attract people to us and for power? Biblically, a truly humble servant of God serves and such a person hardly has any desire to be recognized by man (Matthew 6:1-4). While it is acceptable to give some of our money for the work of the Lord, we are also commanded scripturally to minister to those around us (Galatians 5:13). While using your money to support the work of God is an acceptable offering, how about us being the living sacrifice? (Romans 12:1-2, Luke 14, Acts 4 & 5).

Since the establishment of this ministry, we have been ministering to many believers who are struggling with some sinful habits. In helping me to minister to some of them, the Lord told us that their suffering is self-inflicted, with disobedience and a lack of faith playing a major part in their suffering. The evil desires and cravings feast on them, and they are being smitten by the weakness of the flesh, leading to disobedience (1 Peter 1:13-14). My godly advice to those who are unable to shake off bad habits is this: spend time daily reading the word of God and praying. As I personally discovered, if you do this, you will experience deliverance and the Lord will impart fruit in you for service. When we overcome tests and trials we receive more faith and fruit of the Spirit (1 Peter 1:6-7).

Today, the apostasy of the prosperity teaching only feeds the younger believers God's promises without preparing them for real service through suffering. As it is, suffering produces character and character produces faith and it sustains with endurance (Romans 5:3-5). The Holy Spirit, who is our Helper, uses our knowledge of the Word of God. He convicts us so that we obey the Lord, and through our obedience, we are being pruned to bear fruit (John 15:1-2).

Trials to Test our Faith and Make us Dependent on God

I will now share some practical test we endured as a ministry and a family. We are not sharing this to attract attention to ourselves nor do we seek pity; instead, we are sharing this to encourage you and to let you know that the Lord is using tests to impart fruits of service leading to obedience.

Initially, we would like to use the word "suffering" in explaining some of our experiences. This was new a territory in our Christian lives, and we experienced some degree of pain, rejection and discomfort. Previously when we did ministry work, we did so with ease, without any kind of pressure or discomfort. However, similar to the Bible examples we cited above when the Lord gave us a test, a lot of people started withdrawing from us. It was like separating the faithful from the unfaithful. The believers who did not have faith thought that what we were doing by witnessing late at night and praying till late was both impractical and 'ridiculous'. In our obedience, we acted by faith and we persevered patiently until we could understand what the Lord was doing. Below we briefly detail the various tests from the Lord. As you keep reading, put yourself in our shoes: Do you think you would be able to endure?

The Test of Late Night to Midnight Prayers

In November 2010, the Lord put my wife and me through a prayer and fast test for a full month. He told us through Charis that we must fast for a month and besides our normal daily prayers, we were to start with intercessory prayers from 11:30 PM every night. During this time of devotion, the Lord commanded that our children not be home when we pray. In other words, we should have no one disturbing us. The Lord did, however, allow us to spend some time daily with our daughters and just before dark we would take them to my mother-in-law who agreed to look after them. Our Sunday evening prayer times was especially meant to start from midnight. My wife and I agreed on a list of things to pray for weekly. As an encouragement to the husband and wife who are serving the Lord, praying together holds lasting peace in the family bond and it also gives greater breakthrough in family matters and problems. The Lord did not forewarn us that we would be attacked by the devil, but He promised us protection. At first, we did not realize what He was referring to. We only realized later that He would protect us from Satan's attacks, and indeed, fulfilled this promise.

As we labored in these late night prayers, we experienced various attacks against our bodies and minds. At times, fatigue and sleepiness would set in, and we further experienced heavy attacks against our bodies, leaving us with feelings of deep discomfort. It felt as if our bodies were being tormented, and we had sleepiness and numbness. We felt as if we had no control over our bodies, and we sensed evil in our room with things making a crackling sound. There was a spirit of slumber too, causing me or my wife to fall into a deep sleep while still praying. We only realized this after being awakened by a strong hand from the Lord. As we continued, we would walk in our bedroom praying, sitting or lying down; and I at times would crawl on the floor trying my best to shake off the uncontrollable feeling of discomfort. To best describe that feeling, it was a restlessness, partial numbness and very irritating sensation affecting both the body and the mind. I knew my soul was troubled by this pressure. This attack from Satan, which included pain, fatigue, and discomfort to my body, was meant to discourage us from praying. It seemed that his attacks were particularly elevated on Sunday evenings. Our every longing was the completion of this task and, in the end, the Lord gave us the strength to overcome. This test brought about a great sense of deliverance from our own troubles. About three days after being on this assignment of fasting and prayer, the Lord commanded us, along with our fourteen prayer partners to pray for two weeks gathering together every night. These fourteen prayer partners were people the Lord asked us to find and pray with us, and He had given us one week to find them.

As a result of this late night prayer test, some women experienced persecution through their unsaved husbands. While others, whose husbands were saved, were pressured to stay at home using the "wife must submit" Scripture (Ephesians 5:22), and some others were not interested. To clarify the Scripture on submission, the only time we must not submit to man's authority is when we must obey God (Proverbs 29:25; Acts 5:29).

In commanding these late night prayers, the Lord purposely did this to assess our attitude towards prayer and our obedience to Him. Let's be honest: there are Christians who enjoy praying for their own needs but too busy to attend combatant or intercessory prayers for the good of others. They prefer being comfortable, but the Lord duly rewards the discomfort He allows us to face for the benefit of His Kingdom. As in our situation, many of the brethren who left due to the various pressures they had, re-joined their old habits of watching TV while restricting themselves to only Sunday services, without any active participating in witnessing or other affairs of the body.

After we completed this course of prayers over five weeks, the Lord needed my wife and me to get twenty people to pray with us every Saturday night while He would send us out to witness in our community every Friday night. He told Charis that we must start witnessing from 8:30 PM until about 11:30 PM. From the original twenty people, only six obeyed and joined me and my wife. We armed ourselves with prayer and some tracts; handing them out to everyone we came across on the streets. Because it was too late for us to knock on people's doors, we also placed tracts in their postboxes and on their fences.

This was hitherto an unknown experience and we put our trust in the Lord, who protected us from dogs, thugs, and fear. We understood later that the Lord was targeting youngsters in our community who were either on drugs, clubbing and those going and sitting in the pubs to drink liquor. In our drive to 'impress' the Lord, we also went fearlessly into these pubs, handing out tracts while witnessing to the patrons. I was the only man witnessing with six very brave women, who left their husbands and children at home and gave up early sleep to chase souls for the Kingdom of God. This test went on for about six weeks until the Lord changed the times to our current witnessing time which was from 7:30 PM to 10:00 PM every Friday evening.

A Full Month of Witnessing and Fasting

In August 2011, the Lord told Charis: *"I have a big task for your mother and father and the witnessing team on Monday"*. When the Lord came that Monday, He said: *"The witnessing team must witness and fast for a full month starting tomorrow (Tuesday, August 2011) in (indicating the area) from 8:00 AM to 10:00 PM every day. Your father may only witness with the team when he is off"*. This message caught all of us off-guard and we did not have enough money for car fuel expenses and gospel tracts to go out witnessing. We called a meeting and as a team of seven, we discussed the task, planned and prayed while checking our resources. We ordered additional tracts from a local supplier and also requested for tracts and donations online from some faithful brethren. As a ministry, we give glory to the Lord for the believers who responded by faith, obedience and discernment by helping us in our hour of testing. Their response came as a great encouragement to us and to us, all these precious Christian brothers and sisters were united in purpose. Now may the Lord bless them with everlasting life and comfort them in their struggle of faith.

During our witnessing for the month, we were greeted by scorching heat during the day and bitter cold some nights, along with the fear of dogs and thugs since we were witnessing in a community where we were not known. Many times we also went witnessing while fighting hunger pangs, and we were tortured by exhaustion, fatigue and rejection. The Lord opened the hearts of some residents to open their homes to us to use their toilet facilities as we went along. We love our country and it is not my intention to use this book to speak down on our country, but the reality is, crime is a problem that affects us all. Every area has thugs and their share of gangsters. Although we feared for our safety, especially during the night, we obeyed the Lord and persevered by faith. Being all alone with mostly women, the Lord faithfully watched over us and protected us. In seeing us patrolling their streets, some residents mistook us for either night watchmen or villains, so as we approached them to witness and hand them tracts, some would run away thinking we intended to harm them.

In my absence, while I was at work, my wife and the rest of the team, all women, continued and went out witnessing all by themselves and nothing harmful happened to them. Praise be to God! As a challenge, we often ran out of tracts, but this did not deter us from witnessing. We would decide to witness door to door using our Bibles only and reserving whatever tracts remained to witness at night; we placed them in post-boxes, fences or slipped them under doors. Since it is a bit risky and somewhat odd to knock on people's doors after 7:00 PM, we resorted to witnessing in lighted areas, like petrol stations and frequent hangout places.

Furthermore, we honestly thought we could do with some rest so we asked the Lord about our corporate prayers and weekly services. Instead, He regarded this work as fundamentally important and suspended our prayers until we finished this task. During the short breaks we had, we did short prayers which were our lifeline. As a team, we prayed in turns for about five minutes before leaving for witnessing. As unpleasant it is to say, frustration got the better of some of us, resulting in bitter feuds, but the Lord held us together, encouraging and rebuking the faithless. Geographically, this was a very large area, and we walked very long distances with some houses located sporadically.

Kindly allow me to share briefly my observation regarding the attitudes of some Christians including pastors. The church today uses the Sunday pulpit routine as an excuse not to witness to the unsaved. While enriching themselves with the tithes and offerings, pastors preach every week to the same people who ought to be witnesses themselves! What has become of servants called to serve if they only want to be leaders? (Matthew 20:26) Will the church become silent with the Gospel and allow the tyranny of the devil to use world leaders and evil men to silence us and make us feel ashamed of the gospel? The richness of our Christian history does not allow for silence, but bold preaching (Acts 18:9).

There is not enough time to mention every test we went through including personal test, but I tried to be brief. In addition, the Lord advised that we testify about this to highlight the importance of soul-winning and the need of the gospel to save sinners. My wife was about a month pregnant during our witnessing campaign in Orange Farm, south of Johannesburg. She never used her pregnancy as an excuse not to witness; in fact, the Lord encouraged her to witness with us until the last week before the baby was due to be delivered.

She herself was very eager to go witnessing. Although I was concerned, I leaned on the Lord's assurances, and so supported her efforts.

After my wife gave birth, the Lord gave us a new test: we were to have a deliverance service during our Wednesday services from 6:00 PM to 2:00 AM. Inside I grumbled: "Lord how could you choose this time for deliverance? Our baby daughter is only three days old and she needs her mother!" Although I was troubled, the Lord knew my thoughts, so we obeyed. This was a deliverance session, so no children were allowed. We made arrangements to take the baby and our other daughters to my mother in law's place until after our deliverance service which ended 2:00 AM. On another occasion of testing when our little girl Cailin was about three weeks old, my wife longed to witness with me and the team. The Lord saw her heart's desire and allowed her to join us on the witnessing field after the Lord gave us a new witnessing area to cover. My wife took the baby along, nursing her while witnessing. In concluding this testimony, my wife did not rest from service after she gave birth. After two weeks she was back full time in ministry work and during these times, we left our children in the care of my mother-in-law. Bless her heart! We pray that this testimony will move you into action.

The Lord bless you to pass all trials and tests. May He protect you and help you resist and overcome the enemy to the end. Amen!

CHAPTER 11

Short Vision of People Left Behind

On September 5, 2015, I had a short vision relating to some things that people would experience after the rapture occurs. As for how long after the rapture these things would happen, I do not know; I'm only sharing what I saw. I would also like to add that this is not a complete vision that chronicles all the events that would happen after the rapture. I was only shown partially things to come. This vision is true and trustworthy; it is a warning for people to wake up immediately and make right with God.

In the vision, it was as if I was invisible; I could see people, but they could neither see me nor recognize me. It was as if I was given "binoculars" to clearly see what people were doing, but I could also hear them talking. The first group I saw was a group of young women who were standing almost naked and inviting men to them. The understanding I received is that many of them were high on drugs and that addiction had driven them to prostitution in order to survive and maintain their drug habits. The vision then changed as I followed two men who went into a store to buy something. I could not see what they were buying, but there were other people waiting to go inside. When they came out, I heard them complaining about the high prices and how expensive the item they needed was. It was a "take it or leave it" situation, as the demand for basic items outweighed the supply, and so prices were high. As I followed them looking through the binoculars, I thought they could go to another shop, but then I saw that many business places were closed. As far as I could see, people were competing to get to grocery stores and buy whatever they could. I could see the worry, sadness and the worsening physical condition of some people as they could not find open stores. The two men I had followed seemed to have carried some hard currency, but they disappeared without having had enough money for the thing(s) they wanted. As they disappeared, I heard a song playing, *"Aaaaaahhh, we've been left behind!"*

Yes, this is the song that worldly artists will sing in sympathy to the situation after the rapture. This song and vision bothered me greatly. This was the end of the vision.

Basic Interpretation of the Vision

The Lord is showing us that shortly after the rapture, there will be severe economic hardship and suffering. People will resort to desperate measures to survive, and many will be left unemployed as several businesses will close due to economic failure. People will compete to get basic foodstuffs, and many will not have enough money to afford the basics, or rather that the value of their money will be almost worthless. Our advice today for you is to please repent and come to Christ. Obey Him and follow Him faithfully daily and you will have nothing to fear—not even the great time of testing that the Lord promised would come on the whole world (Revelation 3:10). Be ready, for the Lord is coming really soon!

CHAPTER 12

Prayer of Repentance

We would like to conclude by inviting you to make Jesus your Lord and Savior. He loves you very much and the messages He has given us are for you.

If you want to turn from your present way of life, please pray the prayer below from your heart by faith. God will listen and save you from Hell. After you have prayed in repentance, kindly follow the instructions below to grow in truth, obedience and bear spiritual fruit for service. This short prayer can change your life forever!

Heavenly Father, I bow my head in submission to your will and admit that I am a sinner, destined for HELL if I die without having accepted Jesus Christ as my eternal Lord and Savior. I acknowledge that I cannot save myself and I need a redeemer. I completely repent of my sins and put my faith in the blood of the Lord Jesus Christ shed for my sins on the cross. I NOW accept Jesus Christ as my Savior. Lord Jesus, please fill me with your Holy Spirit. I trust that You will appear soon to take me to Heaven for all eternity. In Jesus' name, AMEN.

After you have prayed this prayer, we encourage you to be a faithful believer by doing the "Duties of a True Born Again Christian" especially, reading your Bible daily *(Joshua 1:8; 1 Peter 2:2)*, praying three or more times per day *(Daniel 6:10; Psalm 55:17)*, and Witnessing *(Mark 16:15)*. Be obedient and live the Word!

More Books to Come!

God willing, we will make more teachings available in book format. We also post messages every week on our website and share some of the visions that the Lord reveals to us as He wills.

In Book 2, we will share more warnings and revelations from the Lord, as well as some visions of hell and the rapture.

Please visit our website:

http://www.preparingforthekingdom.com

The Van Rooyen Family

From left to right: Desiree, Glenn, Claudia, Charis and Jaydeen.
Front: Cailin

About the Author

Glenn K van Rooyen first committed his life to the Lord Jesus Christ in February 1990. In 1992, Brother Glenn received a personal visitation from the Lord Jesus Christ. After the Lord showed him the marks of the cross on His right hand, he proceeded to ask the Lord some questions, and in response, the Lord Jesus referred him to the Bible as the only source of Truth.

After backsliding for more than ten years, Brother Glenn recommitted his life to the Lord in January 2008 following severe hardships. After he started faithfully seeking the Lord again, he and his wife, along with their first-born daughter, started a home fellowship for the family in 2009. After being invited by their local church to participate in a seven-day fast in January 2010, the Lord Jesus Christ gloriously appeared to his then nine-year-old daughter Charis and said, "*I am your Lord Jesus Christ and I will appear to you in visions and give you messages and you must tell your father and I love My children.*"

This was the beginning of the Lord's visits to this family which spanned over a period of more than four years. The Lord visited almost every night, giving them teachings and visions. This is what we share with you in this first book and subsequent titles which will follow.

www.preparingforthekingdom.com

www.ingramcontent.com/pod-product-compliance
Lightning Source LLC
Chambersburg PA
CBHW070527030426
42337CB00016B/2132